Fo

How it began, Leannah's love of entertaining...

When I was a very young child I cooked bacon, eggs and made toast for my teddy bear and dolls. In the 1940's I had a small electric stove with an oven, tucked away in the corner of my mother's kitchen. After "feeding" my bear and dolls I would enjoy eating the food. I still have the bear and three little iron skillets that I used (see page 6) and treasure them dearly. The skillets are on display in my kitchen and I adore showing them off!

My parents had a summer home in Mobile, Alabama on Dog River, a branch of Mobile Bay, off the Gulf of Mexico. As I was growing up I watched my Mom and Dad entertain many people. Most of the time it was on the wharf, with hungry and wet folks just coming in from a swim or boat ride. My mom (better known as Honey) taught me how to feed a crowd on a "shoe string". This was done with a can of corned beef, several loaves of bread, homemade peanut butter cookies and lemonade. Honey would make a large corned beef salad (recipe on page 62) and spread on the bread for sandwiches.

At eleven years of age I was an active Girl Scout, working on my "cooking" badge. I had to cook something from a recipe, all by myself. This cooking fete was Honey's Peanut Butter Cookies (recipe on page 66). I attribute my art of cooking and entertaining to my mother, a real friend, as well as my teacher.

My first large party, accomplished with the help of my first cousin, was a surprise party for my Mom and Dad. It was their twenty-fifth wedding anniversary, September 23, 1950. This was a casual party at our summer home, with relatives and close friends in attendance. I served (you guessed right) corned beef salad sandwiches, peanut butter cookies, nuts, mints and cake. The beverages were punch and cola-flavored carbonated beverage. I was seventeen years old and I admit it was scary but fun to "pull off" this successful party.

The rest of this book will be filled with other "stories" as well as chapters full of different kinds of parties that I have lovingly hosted through the years. Recipes for each party are printed at the end of each chapter. Also for easy reference, recipes are listed alphabetically, by category with page numbers, in an index at the back of the book.

As the title states..."The Three E's to Entertaining: Easy, Economical and Enjoyable," you will see that my style of entertaining has always been done economically and with ease. Bringing people together and feeding them are among my favorite things to do. I call that sheer enjoyment!

Author's Acknowledgement

Greatest thanks to my devoted husband
of forty-seven years, Lyman Faith Holland, Jr.
and my dear friend Sophia H. Clikas,
who inspired me to write this book.

In loving memory of my mother,
Adelaide Ulbricht Platt;
my father, Robert Turner Platt, Sr.
and my maternal grandmother,
Leannah Thrasher Ulbricht.
Their persistence and positive attitude
live on through me.

ISBN 0-9709681-0-8

Graphic design and illustration by
Wise Design, Michelle B. Wise, Mobile, Alabama

Printed in the United States of America
THE WIMMER COMPANIES
Memphis, TN

About the Author

Leannah Louise Platt was born, raised and has lived in Mobile, Alabama all her life. She is married to an attorney, Lyman Faith Holland, Jr. and they have a grown son, Lyman "Buddy" Faith Holland, III; and daughter, Laura Leannah Smith.

Community service has been a part of Leannah's life for over forty years. She was one of the organizers and first woman volunteer of the America's Junior Miss Program, holding the position of assistant to the producer for 20 years. She served as president of the Mobile College Auxiliary, the Mobile Symphony League, the Mobile County Bar Auxiliary and city chairman of the Mobile County Mother's March of Dimes.

She has volunteered with the American Red Cross for over 36 years. Leannah is an active member of the Historic Mobile Preservation Society, Art Patrons League, Mobile Symphony League and the Penelope House (Shelter for Battered Women.) She not only contributes her time as a volunteer with these organizations, but is currently serving on the board of directors for the Art Patrons League, Mobile Symphony, Mobile Symphony League and the Penelope House.

In addition to her volunteer service, Leannah's family continues to have priority in her life. She has remained a very devoted wife, mother and grandmother to her five grandsons, Lee, Luke, Len Allen, Will and Foster.

Leannah is never too busy for her family, church, friends and organizations to entertain and give parties. She is known as the "hostess with the mostest". Entertaining is her "cup of tea".

Many times, throughout the years, she has been asked to go into the catering business. She answers very hurriedly "thank you, but no thank you because that wouldn't be fun." So when one of her close friends insisted she write a book, she decided to do so. Now you will learn her secrets to successful entertaining!

In writing this book she hopes to help newlyweds and people of all ages feel the same way she does...give a party without all the hassle and enjoy every moment from beginning to end.

Leannah's lifetime teddy bear and three little iron skillets, on display in her home today.

Table of Contents

Preparations for Entertaining

I. Find a Party to Give

It takes a reason or special occasion to have a party. I am constantly on the lookout for a "reason" and volunteer often. When I hear that a friend is having a wedding in the family or a baby due, I offer to give them a party. When someone close to me is having a special occasion, such as a birthday or anniversary, I am delighted to have this opportunity to entertain. With my church, organizations involving the arts, and my community, there are many times that I am needed to host a meeting or give a party. That is step one, find a party to give.

II. Plan the Event

The key for a successful event is to be creative and organized. Start planning months in advance, write down ideas about the kind of party, invitations, guest list, date and time. I enjoy having parties in my home. Whether it is a small or large event, I really love cooking the food myself, and have never used a caterer.

III. Invitations

After the date and time are selected, invitations are always sent out two weeks before the event. When I am having a small party I extend my invitation over the telephone. This gives you an accurate count of the number of guests. But when you mail out invitations (I always put "regrets only" on them) to a large group it is hard to get an exact number that will attend. I find many people wait until the last minute to call you. Sometimes people are sick the day of the party and can't come. So, to keep from worrying, I always prepare more food than I need. It is better to have leftovers than run out of food.

IV. Select Menu

The next step is to go through my personal files or cookbooks, and select the perfect recipes. I try to use the ones that are economical, as well as, easy to prepare; preferably foods that can be prepared in advance, frozen, or made several days before the event.

V. Decorations and Table Setting

After the menu has been established I work on planning the decorations, china, flatware, drinking glasses and table linens to be used.

VI. Kitchen Help

For some parties I hire an assistant to help me in the kitchen, but for others I use close friends who enjoy doing this. There are occasions when I handle it alone. It all depends on what kind of party and how many guests will be attending. These people should be engaged early.

VII. Final Preparations

Several weeks before the party I gather all my supplies for decorations (descriptions and helps on decorating are listed in each chapter) and setups (tables, chairs, china, napkins etc.).

Four days before the event I clean my home or have it cleaned.

Three days before the event I grocery shop and organize the nonperishable items in order, with recipes on the kitchen counter. The rest of the ingredients are placed in the refrigerator in stacks, marked according to the dishes to be prepared.

Two days before the event I cook all the foods that I can. Some of the recipes may be prepared a month in advance and frozen. These will be noted in the different chapters.

One day before the fete I set the table or tables, depending on the type of party, and decorate the house. I continue cooking on the day before the party.

The last day I finish the final decorations and complete the cooking. I always allow myself several hours to shower, dress and relax before the party begins. Then it is time to light the candles, set the food and beverages out and enjoy the party!

Notes

Chapter 1

First Meal for In-Laws

Rice?
What to prepare?
Roast?
?
Potatoes?
Ham?
???
???
Happy Anniversary
Happy Anniversary
POTATOES

Chapter 1

First Meal for In-Laws

MENU

Grandmother Leannah's Congealed Salad
Honey's Baked Pork Chops
Honey's Scalloped Potatoes
Green Beans
Rolls
Lemon Meringue Icebox Pie

Relax and calm your anxieties by choosing an easy menu to prepare so you can enjoy your first dinner party honoring your in-laws. What did I choose? My Grandmother Leannah's Congealed Salad, Honey's Baked Pork Chops and Scalloped Potatoes, green beans, rolls (purchased) and Lemon Meringue Icebox Pie with coffee and tea. The recipes are listed on the following pages.

Now isn't that easy? Also very good! My mother-in-law even asked for the recipes which I was happy to share. Do you want to know about the table setting? It was very basic and plain. Newlyweds, long ago, used their best china and silver and crystal for special occasions, but were limited to the linens and flower arrangements due to living on a tight budget. Therefore, my table setting for four, that first meal for my in-laws, was pretty but simple. But I enjoyed every minute and Lyman was proud of me for doing this for his parents.

GRANDMOTHER LEANNAH'S CONGEALED SALAD

(A favorite recipe from Leannah's grandmother, for whom she was named!)

1 (3-ounce) gelatin, any flavor
1 cup boiling water
1 (3-ounce) cream cheese
1 (8-ounce) can crushed pineapple, drained
(You may use any 8-ounce can of fruit such as pear halves, peach slices, or fruit cocktail. Drain all and chop.)
3/4 cup cold water

In a 6x9-inch pan or 1-quart container (which has been sprayed with vegetable cooking spray) empty the gelatin into the pan. Pour the boiling water over the gelatin and stir until dissolved. While hot, place the cream cheese in the dish and stir with a fork until all of it is broken up into small pieces. Add one of the drained fruits (make sure the peaches or pears are diced) and stir. Pour the 3/4 cup of cold water over all and stir until well blended. Place in the refrigerator to congeal. After firm, cover with plastic wrap. This can be made days before the party. When ready to serve, cut into squares and place on lettuce, on salad plates. A cherry or peach slice may be added to the top for garnish. This gelatin salad can also be poured into a 1-quart mold or 6 (small) individual molds.

For the first meal for in-laws, I used lime gelatin with crushed pineapple. That is still a favorite with my family today. The next most popular one is with lemon gelatin and crushed pineapple.

You can make so many different salads with this one recipe from the variety of gelatin flavors and fruits. It is so much fun to try them all!

NOTE: *To enlarge this recipe, to serve more people, follow the same instructions but use the 6-ounce size gelatin, 2 cups boiling water, 8-ounce size cream cheese and fruit. Add 1 1/2 cups cold water and use a 2-quart container or mold. When using molds for either the small or large recipe, mix the ingredients in a bowl and pour into the molds.*

HONEY'S BAKED PORK CHOPS

Pork chops – center cut, approximately ¾ inches thick (one per person)
Water
Catsup

Spray your baking container with vegetable cooking spray (I use different sizes of ovenproof glass dishes, depending on the number of chops I am cooking.) Lay pork chops in bottom of baking dish. Pour enough water to measure halfway up the sides of the chops. Cover tops of chops with catsup and aluminum foil. Bake at 375° for one hour. Check water level after 30 minutes to make sure there is enough water left. Remove aluminum foil cover for the last 10 minutes to brown chops.

NOTE: Always use hot water when adding to a hot ovenproof glass dish so it won't break. Keep water at the halfway "mark" on the sides of the chops.

HONEY'S SCALLOPED POTATOES

(Yield: 6-8 servings)

4 medium sized Irish potatoes
½ cup margarine or butter
salt
pepper
4 tablespoons flour
milk

Wash and peel potatoes and slice thin. Grease a 2-quart baking dish. Place ⅓ of the potatoes in the bottom of the dish. Sprinkle with salt, pepper, flour and pour milk over this to wet the flour. Dot the entire layer with butter. Keep repeating this procedure until all the potatoes are used. Bake, covered, in a preheated 375° oven for 1 to 1½ hours. Remove lid for the last 10 minutes to brown the top.

NOTE: To use this recipe as a main meal add ham or Canadian bacon slices on top of each layer of potatoes, ending up with the potatoes on the top. To feed more people, simply add more potatoes and ham.

GREEN BEANS

3 pounds fresh green beans, washed and snapped
— OR —
4 cans (14-ounce) cut green beans, drained well
4 cups water
2 teaspoons salt
1 teaspoon pepper
3 slices bacon, cut into small pieces
1 medium onion, chopped

Whether using fresh or canned beans, the cooking procedure is the same. Bring the water to a boil in a covered pot, and add salt, pepper, bacon and onion. Then add the beans to the seasoned water.

Bring to a full boil again and lower the heating element to continue cooking at a slow boil, not a simmer. Cook for 1½ hours. Check the water level several times, making sure it hasn't evaporated. I usually have to add water one or two times. You may have to add salt after cooking but sample the finished beans first. It is easier to add than take away! If you prefer crunchy beans, cut the cooking time in half.

LEMON MERINGUE ICEBOX PIE

(Yield: 6 servings)

1 (14-ounce) can sweetened condensed milk
½ cup lemon juice
4 eggs (separate and save)
¼ cup sugar
1 (8-inch) prepared graham cracker pie shell

In medium sized bowl, combine sweetened condensed milk, lemon juice; blend in egg yolks one at a time. Turn into pie shell. Beat the egg whites and slowly add the sugar, until stiff peaks form. Spread over filling and bake at 325° for 15 minutes, until the meringue is golden. Cool the pie and store in refrigerator. Best to make a day ahead of serving. Cover the pie with waxed paper so it doesn't take the top of the meringue off.

Chapter 2

Dinner Parties

Rice?
What to prepare?
?
Roast?
Potatoes?
Ham?
???
???
Happy Anniversary
Happy Anniversary
POTATOES

Chapter 2

Dinner Parties

I. Casual Dinner Party for 8

MENU

Social Hour

Chili Cheese Dip

Party Mix

Jill's Crab Meltaways

Dinner

Grandmother Leannah's Congealed Salad

Wild Rice and Shrimp Casserole

Glazed Carrots

Green Beans

Sour Cream Biscuits

No Crust Coconut Pie

After giving so many dinner parties through the years, I don't know where to begin. I think the best one to start with is a small, casual event. That way if you are giving your first party, or need new ideas, this chapter is for you. Then later on in the chapter you will find help for larger parties, whether a sit-down dinner or buffet.

Did you read "Preparations for Entertaining" on page 9? If not, you need to do so now. That will give you my format for steps to a successful party.

Know the size of your party? Let's base it on eight people. I will "pretend" I am helping you give the party. The date and time have been decided and this party is to honor some out-of-town guests. Other than the two from New Orleans, plus you and your husband, the remainder of the people to attend will be four. Therefore it will be fine to extend your invitation over the phone. This will be an informal supper with friends so be sure and state the dress is casual.

Selecting the menu is next on the agenda. Plan on serving some light appetizers for the "social hour" prior to the sit down dinner. I always schedule a full hour for this gathering, in order to be sure all the guests have arrived before time to serve dinner. For this hour serve Chili Cheese Dip with corn chips, Party Mix and Jill's Crab Meltaways. The beverages will consist of soft drinks, water and a variety of wines.

The dinner party menu consists of Grandmother Leannah's Congealed Salad (page 16), Wild Rice and Shrimp Casserole, Green Beans (page 18), Glazed Carrots, Sour Cream Biscuits and No Crust Coconut Pie. Beverages will be water, with the meal, and coffee, with the dessert. Recipes are listed at end of this section.

Let's think about the decorations and table setting. Even though it is informal, I prefer having the dinner in the dining room. This party is during the winter season and there are no flowers blooming in the garden, so you will need to purchase some flowers. A round 12-inch crystal, or glass bowl would be perfect to use in the center of the table. Always plan on a low arrangement for a sit-down event so the guests can see over it. It would look nice to place some clear glass votive candle holders around the bowl with candles. If you don't have any of these, you need to put them on your list to purchase when you go shopping.

Use evergreens in the bowl, in addition to the flowers. After checking the availability of a bowl, write down what you want to use in the arrangement. To keep the cost minimal, buy a small bouquet of mixed flowers. These may be found in the flower section of the grocery store and are inexpensive. Put a reminder on your list to purchase these flowers two days before the event.

When the dinner is held at other times of the year, flowers from your garden are perfect. I have a shrub that is growing in my yard that is excellent for greenery. It is Cleyera Japonica. Not only is it green year round and never sheds its leaves, the size of the leaf is small, waxy and shiny. This is perfect for garnishes on platters, when giving a buffet, in addition to use as greenery.

Some other greenery suggestions are Japanese yew, boxwood, ivy, ferns and small philodendron. If you are living in a climate where these plants are not accessible year round, I suggest you buy some silk greenery and keep them on hand for making table arrangements. I have even gone into the woods and found perfect trees to pick small limbs. I strip the branches and spray paint them different colors to match my décor. Being creative is fun and saves money.

Looking for a perfect container to put your flowers in? Use items around your home that you never thought about. These are flower pots, watering cans, hat boxes, baskets (place a glass jar or bowl in the bottom for the water), vegetables (pumpkins, different sized squash), watermelons and other fruits, soup tureen, large footed trifle bowl, small punch bowl, cookie jar, china tea pot, footed water goblets, large fruit bowls and just about anything else that holds water. Search and you will be surprised at all the possibilities. Of course, there are a lot of wonderful vases and urns to be used. You can purchase some inexpensive ones and turn them into a beautiful centerpiece.

As far as linens are concerned, I prefer using place mats. I love seeing the beautiful wood showing on top of the table and the mats give a more casual look. They may be used in a formal setting when fancy ones are selected.

Please use sterling silver flatwear, if you have a set, because this makes any occasion seem very special. If not, your stainless flatwear will be great along with everyday china and crystal.

Cloth napkins are the nicest to use, and I keep several different sets available in a variety of colors. I always make sure I choose a color that is compatible with the place mats.

Be on the lookout for napkins and place mats while they are on sale. Most stores put them on sale in July. That is the time to buy several sets and have them on hand for different occasions.

SEVERAL WEEKS BEFORE...

Jill's Crab Meltaways may be made a month in advance and stored in the freezer. Prepare the Party Mix and store in a large glass container with a tight lid. These two recipes are for the "social hour".

FOUR DAYS BEFORE...

The kind of party, date and time have been established, menu selected and invitations extended. Also the ideas for decorations and the table setting have been secured. Since this is a small and casual dinner, there is no need to hire or ask for help in the kitchen. You can handle it alone and do just fine and really enjoy it. This is the day to clean your home and put everything in it's place.

THREE DAYS BEFORE...

All the ingredients are written down and it's time to go shopping. Don't forget to buy candles and wine, if you need them. Upon returning from shopping with all your items, place them on the kitchen counter, alongside the recipes, in the order to be cooked.

Since the menu for this informal dinner party calls for several foods that can be prepared early, start the cooking. It is a good time to make the congealed salad and No Crust Coconut Pie. These will keep very well until the night of the party.The remainder of the dinner party food will be cooked on the next day (two days before the event).

TWO DAYS BEFORE...

Cook the green beans, Glazed Carrots and Wild Rice and Shrimp Casserole. You need to call your grocery store (seafood section) on this day and order your shrimp to be steamed and peeled (this is usually done at no extra charge). Pick them up the afternoon of the day before the dinner party. The store needs a 24-hour notice to have them ready for you. I don't like to wait until the day of the party, so I always order the shrimp to be ready the afternoon before the event. The rice is all that needs to be precooked and kept refrigerated until you assemble the entire shrimp casserole, on the day of the party.

You also need to purchase the flowers on this day and keep them in the refrigerator, in water, until you make your arrangement.The small flower bouquets are also excellent to use on an entrance hall table and in the den, where the "social hour" will take place. Of course, you will have to buy two or three bundles to make these additional arrangements. When my parties are on the week-end I have been fortunate to buy the flowers at a discounted price. They are pulled and marked down as they are classified as "old", but they still look great. Amazing how these little bouquets have decorated my entire house, through the years, for such a low price. I don't claim to be a master gardener or florist expert, but I have fooled a lot of people with my homemade arrangements.

ONE DAY BEFORE...

The fun begins, setting the table! Since you are using your everyday china it makes it easier to clean up, after the party, as you can wash it in the dishwasher, along with your every day crystal. It is best to wash your sterling silver flatwear by hand, but when using your stainless utensils it is fine to put them in the dishwasher. Place the mats and napkins on the table, followed by the flatwear. I keep the plates, glasses and salad plates in the kitchen. They will be filled in the kitchen and carried to the dining room right before the guests are seated.

The table doesn't look too bare since the mats, flatwear, napkins, flowers and candles are colorful and attractive. While setting the table it is all right to place the flower container on the table and a "frog" (small metal disc that has prongs) in the bottom with water and stick the greenery in. This will keep just fine until you add the fresh flowers the next day. It looks very nice to use one of the placemats, that are used at the individual places, under the bowl. The mat protects the table top from the votive candles sitting around the flower arrangement.

Don't forget to fill and place salt and pepper shakers on the table. Step back and take a look and see how everything looks. It is time to double check and make sure you have all the places complete. Now aren't you proud of yourself? Doesn't it look good? Sure it does!

Also remember to set the den for your "social hour". Have an ice bucket next to your soft drinks, a wine opener, glasses and napkins on a side table. Set your appetizer trays in the room. A coffee table would be excellent to use, if you have one. Add napkins to this table.

Remember to go back to the store and pick up the shrimp. Store them in the refrigerator until time to assemble the casserole (the next day) the day of the party.

FINAL DAY...

At last, the final day has arrived and you are almost completely through. You need to take the flowers out of the refrigerator, trim them, throw away any that look wilted, and add to the other containers that have water and greenery in them (throughout the house).

The biscuits and the Chili Cheese Dip are the only food items that haven't been prepared. They are so easy to put together that you can wait until the last minute. The Chili Cheese Dip can be made just minutes before the guests walk in the door. The biscuits taste so yummy when they are served hot out-of-the-oven! Mix and bake them while your guests are in the den, at the conclusion of the "happy hour".

You will be amazed because you have accomplished so much. Looks like you will have extra time to relax and dress. Before you have your "quiet time" it is good to get all your precooked food out of the refrigerator, except the congealed salad and the pies, and let them warm to room temperature (uncovered). Also assemble the rice and shrimp casserole and leave it sitting out.

FIFTEEN MINUTES BEFORE THE GUESTS ARRIVE ...

Preheat your oven and start warming the food. If you have two ovens you may use both, but if not, heat the beans on top of the stove and the remainder in the oven. Start popping the wine corks and fill your ice bucket. Also mix and heat your Chili Cheese Dip in the microwave and place it and your other appetizers in your den.

The party has begun and you should feel happy because everyone is bragging about your food and how pretty your home looks.

TWENTY MINUTES BEFORE DINNER...

Put the biscuits in the preheated oven, the lettuce (already pre-washed) on the salad plates and serve the congealed salad. Place the salad on the table, to the left of each place setting. Fill the glasses with ice and water and light your candles. Also remember to set out the butter dish with butter and a server.

DINNER TIME...

It's time to call your guests into the dining room. They will be so pleased with how lovely everything looks. Have one of your girlfriends come into the kitchen a little ahead of the other guests. As you fill the eight plates have her set them on the dining room table.

After everyone starts eating, you will feel good when different ones compliment your food and ask for the recipes. You are delighted to share them!

This is a good time to bring in the warm biscuits. Place the biscuits in a basket that is lined with a napkin that complements the ones on the table. Let the guests pass and serve themselves.

AFTER DINNER...

When everyone has finished the meal, you may start clearing the table. Usually a lady friend will help you. It is a good idea to ask her to pour the coffee for anyone who desires it. You have already placed the cups and saucers, along with the creamer and sugar bowl (that have been prefilled) on a tray in the kitchen.These are ready to be taken into the dining room. While the coffee is being served, cut the pies and place the slices on the dessert plates (or saucers) with additional forks, and give to the guests. This completes your perfect dinner party of which I hope you loved every minute.

After the guests leave, soak your flatwear, scrape the dishes and put them in the dishwasher to wash. Take all your leftovers and place them in containers and store them in the refrigerator or freezer. You will be glad to use this food another day for a complete meal.

Now it is time to sit down, relax and be proud of yourself, knowing that your friends had a good time and enjoyed your food. Aren't you ready to find another party to give? I am!

PARTY MIX

¾ cup butter or margarine
2 tablespoons Worcestershire sauce
2 teaspoons each: salt, onion salt, celery salt and garlic salt
2 cups each: doughnut-shaped oat cereal, crispy rice cereal squares, crispy wheat cereal squares, stick pretzels
1 cup nuts (any kind)

Melt butter in shallow pan. Add other ingredients and mix well. Bake in preheated 300° oven for one hour. Stir every 10 minutes. When completely cooled, store in air-tight, glass jar.

NOTE: Make weeks in advance.

JILL'S CRAB MELTAWAYS

(Yield: 48 hot canapés)

1 package (6) English muffins
1 (7-ounce) can crabmeat, drained
½ cup margarine, softened
1 (7-ounce) jar sharp, processed cheese spread
2 tablespoons mayonnaise
½ teaspoon seasoned salt
½ teaspoon garlic salt

Cut each muffin half into quarters. Arrange on two cookie trays. Mix all ingredients and spread on muffins. FREEZE. Right before serving put under broiler for 6 minutes. Serve.

NOTE: Make months in advance and freeze.

CHILI CHEESE DIP

1 (15-ounce) jar processed cheese sauce
1 (10.5 ounce) can no bean chili

Mix together in microwaveable bowl. Cover, heat on high for two minutes. Serve with corn chips. Leftovers may be frozen.

WILD RICE AND SHRIMP CASSEROLE

(Yield: 6 servings)

1 (6-ounce) box wild long grain rice mix (Cook according to directions on box.)
1 (10 3/4-ounce) can cream of celery soup
1 (10 3/4-ounce) can cream of mushroom soup
1 pound medium size shrimp, boiled and peeled
1/2 cup cooking white wine

Mix all ingredients with rice. Bake uncovered at 350° for 20 minutes.

NOTE: For 8-10 people double recipe. Use a separate 2-quart dish for second recipe.

GLAZED CARROTS

(Yield: 6-8 servings)

10 carrots, cut in strips
1/2 cup margarine
1/2 cup sugar
1/4 cup water
1/2 teaspoon salt

Place peeled and cut carrots in one quart casserole. Add rest of ingredients. Cover and bake at 375° for one hour.

SOUR CREAM BISCUITS

(Yield: 12 large biscuits, 36 miniature biscuits)

2 cups self-rising flour
1 cup butter, melted (do not use margarine)
1 (8-ounce) sour cream

Mix ingredients by hand and drop in muffin tins. Do not grease pan. Bake at 400° for 25 minutes. Bake miniature biscuits for 15 minutes.

NO CRUST COCONUT PIE

(Yield: Two 9-inch pies)

4 eggs, beaten
1¾ cups sugar
2 cups whole milk
¾ stick margarine, melted
¾ cup flour
1 tablespoon vanilla
2½ cups flaked coconut

Combine all ingredients in a large mixing bowl and stir until well blended. Grease two 9-inch pie plates. Divide mixture evenly into pie plates. Bake at 350° for 30-45 minutes or until golden brown.

***NOTE:** Best to make several days ahead and store, covered, in the refrigerator.*

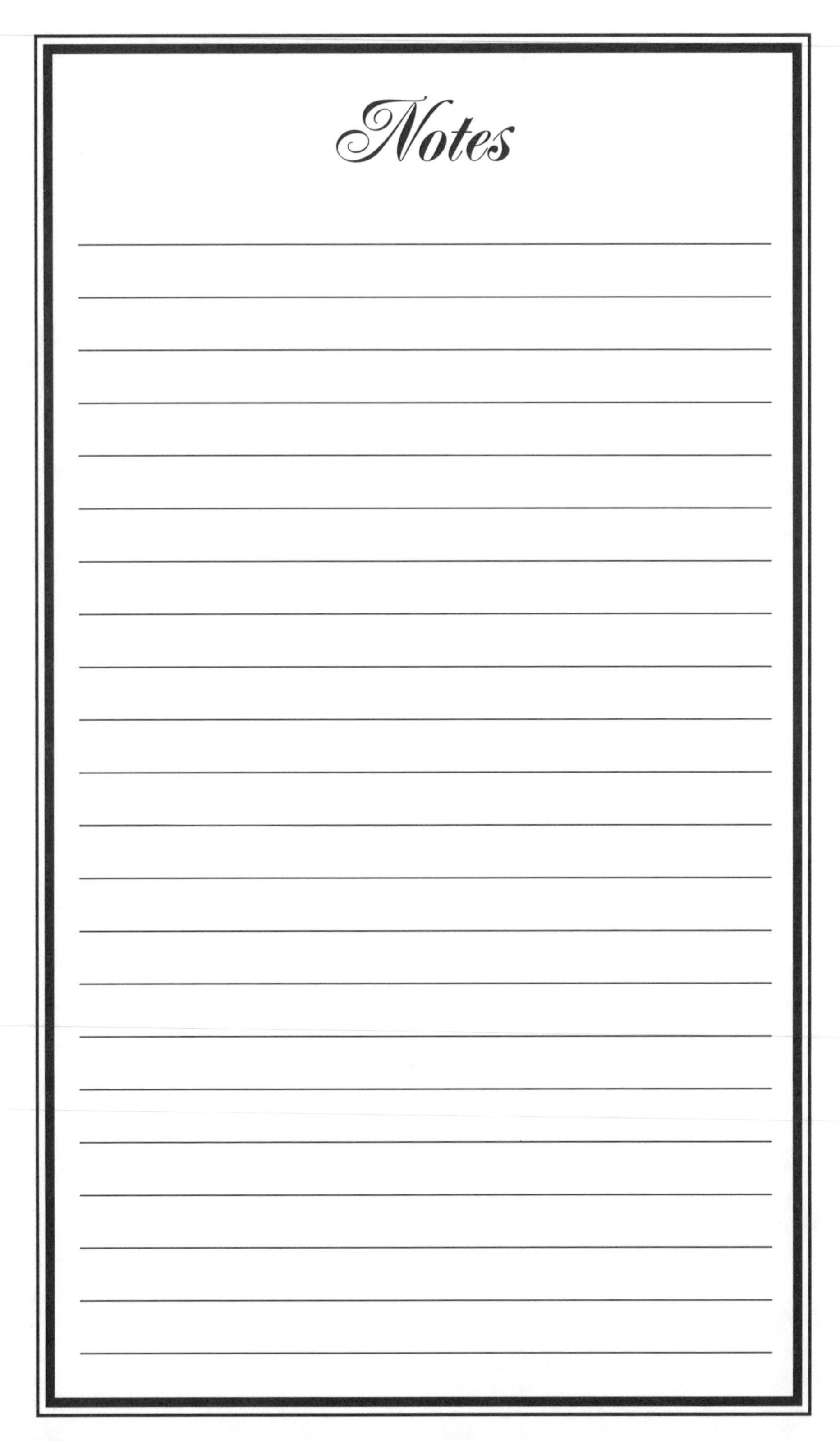
Notes

II. Casual Dinner Party for 12

MENU

Social Hour

Cocktail Oyster Crackers
Dill Dip and Raw Vegetables
Cheese Ball
Wine Punch

Dinner

Cranberry-Pineapple Salad
Chicken and Rice Casserole
English Pea Ragout
Spinach AuGratin
Quick Yeast Rolls
Cherry Cheese Pie

Your casual dinner party for 8 guests was such a success you should try another one, increasing the number to 12. I'm giving you another menu that will prove to be just as easy and delicious. Use wonderful Cocktail Oyster Crackers for the "social hour" and Dill Dip with raw vegetables.

Don't waste your time and money having a large variety of fresh vegetables because I have learned over the years, that raw carrots and celery are the only two that are popular. Choose the ones you like and divide them on your platter with parsley, to make it look nice. The veggies will be dipped into a good dill dip. I like to place my bowl of dip in the center of the vegetables.

Also make a cheese ball for the guests to spread on crackers. Appetizers are supposed to wake up your appetite before the main meal. Therefore these three will be enough and will not be too filling.

In addition to soft drinks during this "gathering time", try a wine punch. This is very economical as well as a joy to make. In case this party is held on a cold night, you may want to use a hot wine punch.

For the dinner party I recommend Cranberry-Pineapple Salad and Chicken and Rice casserole, with English Pea Ragout and Spinach AuGratin. A delicious bread for this menu is Quick Yeast Rolls. For dessert serve Cherry Cheese Pie. These are very easy to make and yummy. Recipes are listed on the following pages.

Get busy and make your lists and have fun planning, decorating (detailed helps are at the beginning of this chapter, pages 21-28) and cooking. You are on your own now and since you were successful with the other party please relax and enjoy it all!

COCKTAIL OYSTER CRACKERS

1 (1-ounce) package powdered buttermilk Ranch salad dressing mix
¾ cup vegetable oil
¼ teaspoon lemon pepper
½ teaspoon dill weed
¼ teaspoon garlic powder
1 (10-ounce) bag of small, round, saltine soup crackers

Combine dressing mix and oil. Add lemon pepper, dill weed and garlic powder. Put crackers on large cookie sheet (with narrow sides) and pour all ingredients over crackers, stirring to coat. Place in a warm oven, 325°, for 15 minutes. Make weeks ahead and store in a closed container.

DILL DIP

(Great with raw veggies or chips)

1 cup mayonnaise
1 cup sour cream
1 tablespoon seasoned salt flavor enhancer
1 tablespoon dill weed
1 tablespoon parsley
1 tablespoon chopped onion
1 teaspoon sugar

Mix together and store covered in the refrigerator. Better next day.

CHEESE BALL

(Make several days ahead)

10 ounces extra sharp Cheddar cheese, grated
2 (8-ounce) cream cheese
¼ cup chopped olives, green or black
2 tablespoons green onion, minced
1 tablespoon garlic powder
2 teaspoons worcestershire sauce
1 teaspoon lemon juice
Chopped nuts

Mix well and form into large ball. Roll in chopped nuts. Serve with crackers and spreaders. Reshape leftover ball and freeze. Ready for next party!

WINE PUNCH

1 part cranberry juice
1 part gingerale
2 parts Chablis wine

Chill juices and wine, pour into punch bowl or pretty pitcher.

HOT WINE PUNCH

2 sticks cinnamon
6 whole cloves
½ cup sugar
2 cups apple cider
2 cups orange juice
2 cups burgundy wine

Tie spices together in cheese cloth. Simmer all together (except wine) for 30 minutes. Then add wine and heat until hot.

CRANBERRY-PINEAPPLE SALAD

(Yield: 12 servings)

2 (3-ounce) packages lemon flavored gelatin
3 cups boiling water
1 (16-ounce) can cranberry sauce
1 cup crushed pineapple, drained
½ cup chopped pecans

Dissolve gelatin in boiling water. Beat cranberry sauce with mixer on low speed. Add cranberry sauce, pineapple and pecans to gelatin. Pour into an 12 x 8 x 2-inch pan and chill until firm. Best to make a day ahead of party. Cut into squares and place on lettuce when serving.

CHICKEN AND RICE CASSEROLE

(Yield: 12 servings)

2 cups uncooked rice
2 (2-ounce) boxes onion soup mix
12 skinless, boneless chicken breast halves, one per person
2 (12-ounce) cans evaporated milk
squeeze margarine

Cook rice. Grease one 3-quart baking dish. Place rice evenly in bottom of dish. Open one box of soup mix (2 envelopes) and sprinkle over rice. Wash chicken and arrange over rice. Pour evaporated milk over all. Squeeze margarine over chicken and sprinkle 2nd box (2 envelopes) of onion soup on chicken. Cover. Bake at 425° for one-half hour. Reduce oven to 225° and bake for one hour.

ENGLISH PEA RAGOUT

(Yield: 6-8 servings)

1 (10 3/4-ounce) can tomato soup
1 (10 3/4-ounce) can cream of mushroom soup
1 (15-ounce) can English peas, drained
3 hard boiled eggs, sliced
1 cup grated cheese

Combine soups and peas. Grease 2-quart casserole dish and put half of the soup/pea mixture, then half of the egg slices, then half of the cheese. Repeat layers. Bake at 350° for 20-25 minutes.

SPINACH AU GRATIN

(Yield: 6 servings)

1 (10-ounce) package chopped spinach
1 tablespoon chopped onion
2 eggs, well beaten
1/2 cup sour cream
salt and pepper to taste

Cook spinach in the microwave with small amount of water and onion for about 10 minutes. Drain and add other ingredients. Bake uncovered at 350° for 30 minutes in a greased 1-quart casserole dish. Make 2 recipes for 12 people.

QUICK YEAST ROLLS

(Yield: 20)

1 package yeast
2 cups hot water
1/4 cup sugar
4 cups self-rising flour
3/4 cup vegetable oil
1 egg

Combine yeast and 2 cups hot water; set aside. Combine sugar and flour in large container with tight-fitting lid. Pour oil, egg and yeast-water over flour; mix thoroughly. Refrigerate for 45 minutes. Spoon into muffin tins that have been sprayed with non-stick vegetable cooking spray. Bake at 425° for 20 minutes. These may be made the day before the party and heated in low oven (covered) before serving.

CHERRY CHEESE PIE

(Make days before party.)

2 (8-ounce) cream cheese
3 eggs
2/3 cup sugar
1 teaspoon vanilla
dash of salt
1 (21-ounce) can cherry pie filling

Cream all above, except cherry pie filling, and pour into two greased 9-inch pie plates. Spoon 1/2 can of cherry pie filling over each pie. Bake at 375° for 30 minutes. Cool and store covered in refrigerator.

III. Buffet Dinner Party

MENU

Social Hour

Barbecued Peanuts

Parmesan Cheese Dip with Raw Vegetables

Smoked Oyster Dip

Dill Pickle Appetizers

Deviled Eggs

Cranberry Sparkle Punch

Dinner

Mixed Green Salad

Peaches

Three Vegetable Casserole

Company Casserole

Rolls

Double Chocolate Brownies

Lemon Squares

After the wonderful dinner party for 12 why not be brave and give a casual buffet dinner party for 35 or 40? Come on, don't chicken out on me! It is fun and a perfect time to honor your boss and co-workers. Or is it your turn to host your supper club? Whatever the reason may be to give the party, it will require long range preparations and thought.

After you have selected the date, time and guest list (always invite more than you plan on attending, due to cancellations) it will be necessary to have invitations printed for such a large group.

If you are "gifted" on the computer it would save you money to go in that direction. So put your mind to work and if you can't produce the invitations maybe you have a friend or relative that will be willing to help.

Your next concern will be the plan of serving and set ups. Parties this size usually require borrowing six foot folding tables from friends or relatives. The "social hour" for a large group is great to have outdoors, on a patio or deck. You never know what to expect when it comes to the weather, so you will need a back-up plan. You may use a large room inside, such as a great room or den, for the gathering.

Set up your tables opposite from each other and place the drinks on one and the appetizers on the other. For this large group I would prepare plain punch and "spiked" punch. The plain punch is Cranberry Sparkle Punch and when you add white rum it is "spiked".

Serve at least five appetizers. I recommend Barbecued Peanuts, Smoked Oyster Dip with corn chips, deviled eggs, a raw vegetable tray using Parmesan Cheese Dip and Dill Pickle Appetizers.

For the main buffet serve mixed green salad, canned sliced peaches (purchase a large 6-pound can, chill and drain well). Three Vegetable Casserole (make 4 recipes), Company Casserole (make 6 recipes) and dinner rolls (purchase small ones that come 24 to a package) and brush the tops with butter before heating. The desserts are Double Chocolate Brownies and Lemon Squares. Recipes are at the end of this section.

If you have an island in your kitchen, use this to place your buffet dinner on, or use a buffet or sideboard in your dining room. With this many people I suggest you use large plastic disposable plates, placing them at the beginning of your line. If the plastic bothers you, feel free to borrow "everyday" china plates. It is OK that the china doesn't match.

The ideal setup would be a double line on a kitchen island, and have your breakfast room table and dining room table pre-set with flatwear and napkins.I don't like to use plastic forks (no knives needed with this menu) so I borrow stainless steel forks from relatives or close friends to have enough for the 40 guests.

Your cloth napkins may be mismatched also. It looks nice when you pre-set the tables, to have all the napkins matching in the dining room as well as the ones in the breakfast room.

You are going to need more tables, other than the dining room and breakfast room, to accommodate your guests. I use card tables placed throughout the house. You may need to ask your close friends or relatives for folding tables and chairs. People prefer sitting at a table and not having to balance their food, so it is worth all your hard work to furnish tables for your guests.

Water, ice and large plastic cups should be positioned on a kitchen table or counter, near the food line. All the food (including the pick-up desserts) go on the one plate so they can pour and carry their own water cup. I also place a large coffee maker, full of hot coffee (next to the water) with small styrofoam cups and cream and sugar.

I take 3x5-inch white cards and write down the food items (one per card) along with the name of the serving container to be used, and lay them down on the island, tables or whatever is going to be used. That way I can see if I have room for everything and keep the cards and use them again the day before the party. I place and leave them until I put the actual food in the spot of the card.

If you will follow this plan, there is no need to have extra help in the kitchen for the buffet. You will have all your food precooked and can place your "social hour" food in position (where the cards are) and continue working on other details in the kitchen. While your guests are enjoying the "gathering time" slip away and go into the kitchen and start placing the main course foods. This method really speeds up your serving as well as helps you remember your great plan.

During the pre-planning, I recommend making a diagram of the rooms that will be used for the eating tables. This gives you a look at how many tables you are going to need and where to place them. If you serve the buffet in the kitchen and use your dining room and breakfast room tables, you may need to put the extra ones in the den, study, living room or hallway.

I can seat 12 in my dining room and 8 in my breakfast room, so I know I need to have 20 places elsewhere. I use card tables that seat 4, so I use 5 of these smaller tables.

Place mats are used on the larger tables but for the five card tables I purchase and use white plastic, disposable cloths. These can be cut to fit the tables and look nice with the assorted colors of dinner plates. Place salt and pepper shakers on each table. No butter will be needed since the rolls are pre-buttered.

As far as flowers are concerned, I use semi-large arrangements for the two main tables but use small floral displays on the card tables. I have found china soup bowls are a good size to place the greenery and flowers in for those little tables. Don't forget to refer to the beginning of this chapter, in the first section, (pages 21-28) for help on making your own flower arrangements and suggestions for containers.

With all your details worked out about the tables and setups, you can focus on putting your plans into action. It is best to have your list in front of you when calling to borrow different items, writing down the persons name and item to be picked up. You have started early on this so it is a good idea to secure everything and store it all in your garage.

This is where a husband, boyfriend, teenager or relative comes in handy. He can help with the lifting, picking up at the different locations and returning the items. Of course, teenagers love to receive money and it will be worth the cost to obtain this help.

After completing your lists and shopping, you are ready to start your cooking. Remember to check the recipes and find the ones that can be prepared days and weeks in advance.

Then the "count down" for the rest of your plans will fall into place. Continue following the pattern already established for your last two parties and it will be a joy to accomplish this large, casual, buffet dinner.

I will say it again, be organized, creative and have fun, as you accomplish another successful party!

BARBEQUED PEANUTS

1 tablespoon liquid smoke
1 tablespoon Worcestershire sauce
1/3 cup water
2 cups salted (canned) peanuts
1 tablespoon butter, melted
1/4 teaspoon garlic salt

Combine liquid smoke, Worcestershire sauce and water in small saucepan; bring to a boil. Add peanuts; let stand 30 minutes. Drain off liquid, spread nuts in shallow baking pan and bake at 250° for one hour. Toss nuts with butter and drain on paper towels. Sprinkle with garlic salt. After thoroughly cooled and drained it is good to store them in the peanut can (or jar) that they came in. These may be cooked days before the party.

PARMESAN CHEESE DIP

2 cups sour cream
1 cup shredded sharp Cheddar cheese
1/2 cup parmesan cheese
4 slices bacon, cooked crispy and crumbled
1/4 cup green onion, finely chopped

Combine sour cream and cheeses; mix well. Stir in bacon and onion; chill. Make this recipe 3 times for 40 people.

SMOKED OYSTER DIP

(Yield: 12 servings)

2 (8-ounce) cream cheese
1 teaspoon Worcestershire sauce
2 teaspoons lemon juice
1 cup sour cream
1 (3.7-ounce) can smoked oysters, do not drain

Blend cream cheese with Worcestershire sauce, lemon juice and sour cream. Add oysters and mix well. Serve with corn chips. For a variety, cut out a large hole in the top of a loaf of round bread and scoop it out. Use the bread as a bowl for the oyster dip. Make the recipe 3 times for 40 people.

DILL PICKLE APPETIZER

(Yield: 40 servings)

1 (46-ounce) jar whole dill pickles, drained (not polish or kosher)
1 (8-ounce) cream cheese, softened
1 (3-ounce) package sliced sandwich ham

Select ten of the largest pickles. Cover the entire pickle with a thin layer of cream cheese so that the pickle doesn't show through. Don't put the cheese on the ends. Cut the ham slices the length of each pickle and roll them up. Wrap each one in plastic wrap and lay on a tray in the refrigerator. They can be assembled a week before the party. As the party begins, take out one or two and slice them with a sharp knife (like cutting cookie dough) about 1/4 inch thin. When placed on your serving platter they look like round pinwheels of ham, cheese and pickle. Always a favorite!

NOTE: When you are slicing the two ends off the pickle, save these in a plastic bag in the refrigerator to eat another day. They are uneven and don't look "nice", but they taste good.

DEVILED EGGS

(Yield: 12)

6 hard boiled eggs, cut in half, lengthwise
1/4 cup mustard
1/3 cup mayonnaise
1/4 cup sweet pickle relish, drained
1/4 cup celery, finely chopped
1/4 cup onion, finely chopped
salt and pepper to taste
paprika

Place yolks in bowl and mix with other ingredients. Fill empty egg white "cups" with yellow mixture. Sprinkle with paprika. Chill overnight, covered with waxed paper. Prepare 2 dozen eggs for 40 people.

CRANBERRY SPARKLE PUNCH

(Yield: 24 - 1/2 cup servings)

2 (1-pound) cans jellied cranberry sauce
1 cup frozen orange juice concentrate, thawed and undiluted
½ cup frozen lemon juice, thawed and undiluted
2 cups cranberry juice
4 cups gingerale

In a large mixer bowl, beat cranberry sauce until smooth. Add orange juice concentrate, lemon juice and cranberry juice; blend until thoroughly combined. In punch bowl add precooled gingerale and mix well. Serve immediately with an ice mold made of extra cranberry juice.

NOTE: Double this recipe for 40 people (plain punch). Then for "spiked" punch add 1 cup of white rum for each recipe made of the plain punch. Judge how many recipes of the "spiked punch" to make based on the number of guests that are attending that drink "spiked punch".

MIXED GREEN SALAD WITH OIL AND RED WINE VINEGAR DRESSING

(Yield: 40 servings)

2 heads iceberg lettuce
2 heads boston (red top) lettuce
4 strips of bacon, cooked and broken into small pieces
2 (8-ounce) cans mandarin oranges, drained, cut in half
3 cups vegetable oil
1 cup catsup
1 cup red wine vinegar (with garlic)
1 cup diced onion
1 tablespoon sugar
salt and pepper to taste

Wash, drain and tear up lettuce (day before party) and store in large plastic bags in the refrigerator. Cook bacon and keep in the refrigerator. Mix the last 7 ingredients in a jar and right before serving (after all the other items have been tossed in a large salad bowl) stir well, pour over salad and toss.

THREE VEGETABLE CASSEROLE

(Yield: 8-10 servings)

2 (10-ounce) packages frozen broccoli
2 (10-ounce) packages frozen brussel sprouts
2 (10-ounce) packages frozen cauliflower
2 (10 3/4-ounce) cans cream of mushroom soup, undiluted
1 (2-ounce) box onion soup mix (2 envelopes)
American cheese slices

Cook vegetables according to directions on packages. Layer vegetables and soups in a 3-quart casserole dish. Top with slices of American cheese. Heat uncovered at 325° for 30 minutes.

COMPANY CASSEROLE

(Yield: 4-6 servings)

1 cup uncooked rice
1 (11-ounce) can whole kernel corn, drained
2 (10 3/4-ounce) cans tomato sauce
1 small white onion, chopped
1 pound ground sirloin steak
3 slices bacon, cut into 1½ inch strips
water
salt and pepper

Pour rice in bottom of two-quart greased casserole dish. Pour corn on top of rice. Sprinkle with salt and pepper. Pour one can tomato sauce over this and fill empty can half full of water and also pour over above. Distribute onion over ingredients. Place chopped meat on onion. Sprinkle with salt and pepper. Pour one can tomato sauce over this and fill can 1/4 full of water and pour over meat. Top with bacon pieces and bake covered at 350° for one hour. Remove lid for 15 minutes to brown bacon.

DOUBLE CHOCOLATE BROWNIES

(Yield: 3 dozen)

1¼ cups flour
¼ cup sugar
½ cup margarine, softened
1 (14-ounce) can sweetened condensed milk
¼ cup cocoa
1 egg
1 teaspoon vanilla
½ teaspoon baking powder
1 (8-ounce) milk chocolate bar, broken into chunks
¾ cup chopped nuts

Preheat oven to 350°. Line 9x13-inch baking pan with foil, set aside. In bowl combine 1 cup flour and sugar, cut in butter, until crumbly. Press in bottom of pan. Bake 15 minutes. In another bowl beat milk, cocoa, egg, remaining ¼ cup flour, vanilla and baking powder. Mix chocolate pieces and nuts. Spread over precooked crust. Bake at 350° for 20 minutes, or until set. Cool. Lift out of pan and cut into bars. Make weeks ahead and store covered. For 108 brownies, make recipe 3 times.

LEMON SQUARES

(Yield: 18 squares)

CRUST

1 cup flour, sifted
½ cup butter, melted
¼ cup powdered sugar

Mix and press in grease pan. Bake 350° for 20 minutes.

BATTER

1 cup sugar
½ teaspoon baking powder
2 eggs
2 tablespoons flour
3 tablespoons lemon juice

Mix batter and pour over precooked crust. Bake at 350° for 25 minutes. Remove from oven. Cut in squares while warm. Cool and sprinkle with powdered sugar. These can be made weeks in advance and stored in covered containers.

***NOTE:** 2 recipes fill one 9x13-inch rectangular baking pan and yield 36 squares. One recipe fills a 9-inch square baking pan and yields 18 squares.*

IV. Formal Dinner Party

MENU

Social Hour

Cheese Straws

Seafood Tartlets

Bacon Dip

Cucumber Delights

Champagne Punch

Dinner

Vegetable Cheese Soup

Romaine Salad

Orange Glazed Carrots

Green Rice

Beef Tenderloin with
Marchand de Vin Sauce

Southern Style Bread

Ann's Buttermilk Pie

Now that you are gifted with accomplishing a variety of casual dinners it is time to move forward into the area of formal dinners. We live in a world of casual existence and see it everywhere. But once in awhile you may need to entertain on a formal level. I want to help you learn how to achieve this.

What do you think when you hear the word "formal"? Black tie attire? Could be, but I am referring to coat and tie for men and dressy clothes for ladies. It is exciting to "dress up" occasionally for dinner!

I had this style dinner, in our home, for a retiring Admiral; also a Count and Countess, visiting from Scotland. Talk about thrilling!

After the date and time were established and invitations decided upon (used printed ones) the fun began with the planning. Both of my formal dinners were for 10 people. I decided to begin the evening in our living room and used one of our larger round corner tables for the appetizers. And a smaller table proved good to house a tray with champagne glasses, filled with champagne punch. Appetizers were served on silver trays.

For the "social hour" I served Champagne Punch, Cheese Straws, Seafood Tartlets, Cucumber Delights and Bacon Dip with sesame and cheese snack sticks. For the main dinner I prepared Vegetable Cheese Soup, romaine lettuce with toasted sesame seeds, grated romano cheese and Italian dressing sprinkled on the top, Orange Glazed Carrots, Green Rice, Beef Tenderloin, Marchand de Vin Sauce, Southern Style Bread and Ann's Buttermilk Pie. Recipes are at the end of this section.

For my table in the dining room I used a white linen table cloth, sterling silver flatwear, fine china and crystal goblets. I furnished bread and butter plates at each place with individual silver butter spreaders, along with homemade place cards. The linen napkins were held with silver napkin ring holders. Candles were placed in silver candlesticks on the dining room table and lighted. I arranged the flowers in a footed silver twelve inch round bowl.

I hired a lady to remain in the kitchen and serve the food for the main dinner; although, I had prepared the entire meal. This way I could sit down and enjoy the guests and this made it seem more "formal".

These parties were wonderful and all the guests gave rave reviews about the entire events. I believe I enjoyed it more than anyone, though, as accomplishing a perfect fete leaves you with a great feeling of pride and joy. I highly recommend you entertain with a formal dinner party in the near future!

NOTE: Let me share what my grandmother Leannah taught me about silver when I was a young homemaker. After you polish your silver (should be done months before your party to conserve time) place a cake of camphor gum in with your silver. You can buy it at a pharmacy and leave the cellophane wrapper around the 2 inch block, but make a slit in the paper so the odor is released. Do not let the camphor touch the silver. This helps keep the tarnish from forming so rapidly. You need to have your silver in a closed cabinet or the flatwear in a drawer where the air cannot reach it. The camphor does work and you will be pleased and surprised.

CHEESE STRAWS

(Yield: 3 dozen)

3 cups flour
1/2 teaspoon baking powder
1/4 teaspoon red pepper
1/2 cup margarine
1 cup grated sharp Cheddar cheese
3 tablespoons cold water
dash of salt

Sift flour and baking powder; add pepper. Cut in margarine and cheese. Add water, salt and mix well. Press through cookie press. Bake at 375° for 8-10 minutes .

SEAFOOD TARTLETS

(Yield: 15)

1 (6 ounce) can crabmeat, drained
1 (4.25 ounce) can baby shrimp drained and chopped
1 cup mayonnaise
1/3 cup Parmesan cheese
1/3 cup shredded Swiss cheese
1/3 cup chopped green onion
1/4 teaspoon Worcestershire sauce
4 drops Tabasco sauce
1 package (miniature size) Filo shells
paprika

Put crabmeat and shrimp in a medium sized mixing bowl. Add remaining ingredients. Mix well. Fill shells and sprinkle tops with paprika. Broil (on cookie sheet) for 3 minutes. Cool, then freeze (covered). To serve: preheat oven to 450°, heat frozen tartlets for 7 minutes, and serve.

NOTE: *Make weeks in advance. You may also make several recipes at a time and keep them, all year round, in freezer for last minute guests.*

CUCUMBER DELIGHTS

(Yield: 5 dozen)

5 medium cucumbers
1 (12.5 ounce) can chicken, drained
1 hard boiled egg, finely chopped
1/2 cup mayonnaise
1/4 cup onion, finely chopped
2 tablespoons pecans, toasted and finely chopped
dash of salt and pepper
5 dozen pecan halves, toasted for tops

Wash cucumbers and score all sides with a fork. Cut a dozen slices from each cucumber. Set aside. Mix all ingredients (except 5 dozen roasted pecan halves). Refrigerate 2 hours or more, and right before serving, spread one teaspoon of mixture on each cucumber slice. Place one roasted pecan half on top. Best to make day ahead of event.

BACON DIP

(Yield: $2^{1}/_{3}$ cups)

1 (1-ounce) envelope onion soup mix
2 (8-ounce) sour cream
2 slices bacon, cooked and crumbled

Mix, cover and chill. Serve with sesame and cheese snack sticks.

CHAMPAGNE PUNCH

(Yield: 12 servings)

3/4 cup (6-ounce can) frozen pink lemonade concentrate, thawed and undiluted
1 1/2 cups water
1/4 cup honey
1 fifth champagne, chilled

In punch bowl, combine all ingredients, except champagne; mix well. Add champagne, mix again and serve immediately in chilled champagne glasses.

VEGETABLE CHEESE SOUP

(Yield: 2 quarts)

3 cups water
2 medium potatoes, peel and cut into small cubes
2 chicken bouillon cubes
1/2 (16-ounce) package frozen mixed vegetables (broccoli, carrots, and cauliflower)
1/2 pound processed cheese loaf, chopped
1 (10 3/4-ounce) can cream of chicken soup
1 onion, chopped
pepper, no salt

Cook potatoes in water with onion until almost done. Add the bouillon and vegetables and continue cooking. When vegetables are done add cheese and cream of chicken soup. Stir until blended. Add pepper - no salt.

ORANGE GLAZED CARROTS

(Yield: 6 servings)

2 (8-ounce) packages frozen baby carrots, cooked until tender
1/2 cup plus 4 tablespoons orange juice
1/2 cup maple syrup
4 tablespoons orange marmalade

Stir together juice, syrup and marmalade and boil. Add cooked carrots. Drain before serving.

GREEN RICE

(Yield: 4-6 servings)

3/4 cup chopped green onion
3 tablespoons olive oil
2 cups chicken broth
1/2 cup minced green pepper
1 teaspoon salt
1 cup uncooked rice
1/4 cup chopped parsley
1/4 teaspoon pepper

Cook onion in oil until soft, not brown. Add remaining ingredients, pour into 2-quart casserole. Cover and bake at 350° for 30-45 minutes, or until rice is tender.

SOUTHERN STYLE BREAD

(Yield: 12 servings)

1 cup butter, melted (reserve 1/2 cup)
1 cup milk
1 package yeast
2 eggs
1/2 teaspoon salt
3 cups flour (reserve 1/2 cup)

Mix together everything except 1/2 cup flour and let rise one hour. Add remaining flour and let rise in refrigerator overnight. Drop in greased fluted cake pan by spoonfuls. Pour 1/2 cup of melted butter over bread. Bake at 350° for 30 minutes.

BEEF TENDERLOIN

5 to 6 pound beef tenderloin
butter
garlic salt
salt and pepper

Rub with a paste of butter, garlic salt and pepper. Preheat oven to 450°, cook 25-30 minutes for medium, 20-25 minutes for rare. Serve with Marchand De Vin Sauce.

MARCHAND DE VIN SAUCE

(Cook in microwave. Freezes well or can be refrigerated for several weeks.)

½ cup stick butter
½ cup onion, finely chopped
4 cloves minced garlic
½ cup mushrooms, finely chopped
2 tablespoons flour
½ teaspoon salt
⅛ teaspoon pepper
⅛ teaspoon red pepper
1 cup beef stock
½ cup red wine

Melt butter in a 4 cup glass measuring cup. Saute onion and garlic on high 5 minutes. Add mushrooms, cook on high two minutes. Stir in flour, salt and peppers. Cover with waxed paper and cook on high two minutes. Stir in beef stock and wine. Cover with waxed paper, cook on high 10 minutes. Stir once.

ANN'S BUTTERMILK PIE

1 cup sugar
2 eggs
2 tablespoons butter, melted
2 cups buttermilk
2 tablespoons flour
1 teaspoon lemon extract

Mix by hand in order given. Pour in buttered 10-inch pie plate. Bake at 350° for 50 minutes. Garnish with aerosol whipped dessert topping and a cherry on top.

Notes

Chapter 3

Coffee Parties

Rice?
What to prepare?
?
Roast?
Potatoes?
Ham?
???
???
Happy Anniversary
Happy Anniversary
POTATOES

Chapter 3

Coffee Parties

MENU

Finger Sandwiches
Tortilla Wraps
Sausage Cheese Balls
Broccoli Cornbread Miniature Muffins
Cheese Straws
Party Mix
Frances's Spice Pecans
Assorted Cookies and Cakes
Coffee and Hot Tea
Coffee Punch

Need an explanation? Up until a few years ago these parties were very popular. Today they are rare since so many women are working outside the home. When clubs, civic organizations and churches held meetings in the morning hours they served coffee with tasty goodies. They were known as coffee parties.

Large groups would attend and were served refreshments (buffet style) prior to the meeting. The living room or den was the setting for the meeting and the refreshments were served in the dining room.

Usually a silver service would be used and placed at the end of the table. A large bouquet of flowers adorned the center, with food around the arrangement.

The delicious food was served on silver or crystal trays, with paper (lace) doilies under the food. These doilies may be purchased today in different sizes. Each tray was garnished with greenery, parsley or fresh flowers. Candles were not used as these parties were held in the mornings.

On some occasions coffee parties were held without a business meeting. It would be a time to simply have a party for a friend, welcome a new neighbor, a relative visiting from out-of-town or say "thank you" to someone.

I listed a number of menu possibilities at the beginning of this chapter, but if you want to host a coffee party you will only prepare a limited amount of food. I suggest two different types of finger sandwiches (trim the crust and cut the bread into squares, strips, rounds, hearts or whatever shape you like), a salty item and a variety of sweets.

Place a stack of cloth napkins (approximately 6 inches square), individual china or glass plates and salad forks at one corner of your table. The people in attendance will help themselves to the food. Cups and saucers should be located next to the silver service. It is a good idea to serve hot tea, along with the coffee, since silver service sets have a tea and coffee pot. You will find a good many guests prefer hot tea over coffee and it is nice to have both beverages available.

I have given coffee parties when the weather was warm and prepared coffee punch with vanilla ice cream floating on the top. My recipe serves 50 people and is delicious.

You may not be interested in hosting one of these parties, but the following recipes may be used to supplement other events.

SANDWICHES

EGG SALAD

(Yield: 9 whole, 18 halves, or 3 dozen finger sandwiches)

6 eggs, hard boiled and peeled, remove yolks and set aside, finely chop whites
½ cup celery, finely chopped
1 small onion, finely chopped
⅓ cup (10-ounce) jar sweet pickle relish, drained
½ cup mayonnaise
½ teaspoon salt
¼ teaspoon pepper
¼ cup mustard
1½ loaves (1-pound 4-ounce size) white or whole wheat bread, crusts removed

Mix egg whites, celery, onion, relish, mayonnaise, salt, and pepper in bowl. Mash the yolks with mustard in a separate bowl and add to the first mixture. After mixing well, if too stiff add a little more mayonnaise. Cover and chill overnight. Next day spread on bread. Cut into desired shapes.

*NOTE: To make **Chicken Salad** (quick and easy) use one (12½ ounces) can chicken, drained. Prepare the same way as **Egg Salad**. For **Tuna Salad** (quick and easy) use 2 (6-ounce) cans of tuna fish, drained. Prepare the same way as **Egg Salad**.*

CREAM CHEESE WITH PINEAPPLE ON CRANBERRY/RAISIN BREAD

(Yield: 3 dozen finger sandwiches)

1 (8-ounce) cream cheese, softened
½ (8-ounce) can crushed pineapple, drained
2½ loaves (1 pound loaf) cranberry/raisin bread, crusts removed

Mix well and chill overnight. Spread on bread next day. Make ahead.

HONEY'S CORNED BEEF SALAD

(Yield: 30 whole, 60 halves, or 90 finger sandwiches)

1 (12-ounce) can corned beef
8 eggs, hard boiled and peeled, remove yolks and set aside, finely chop whites
3/4 cup celery, chopped
1 medium sized onion, chopped
1/2 (10-ounce) jar sweet pickle relish, drained
1 1/2 cups mayonnaise
3/4 teaspoon salt
1/2 teaspoon pepper
1/2 cup prepared mustard
3 loaves (1-pound 4-ounce size) whole wheat or white bread, crusts removed for finger sandwiches
celery sprig with leaves (Use as garnish for a mold.)

Break up corned beef in large bowl. Add egg whites, celery, onion, relish, mayonnaise, salt and pepper. Mix well. In separate bowl mix yolks with mustard and blend into the corned beef mixture. If too stiff add a little more mayonnaise. Cover and chill overnight. Next day spread on bread.

NOTE: To make a ***Molded Ball*** *(for cocktail or wine and cheese party) spray a 12 ounce empty plastic container with non-stick vegetable cooking spray and pack the corned beef salad into the container. The next day, run a table knife around the sides of the container and turn the mold onto a platter. For garnish, stick a green leaf (sprig from celery) into the center. Place crackers around the mold, with spreaders. For a variety, use pumpernickel party bread, instead of crackers and have guests make their own open-faced sandwiches.*

DEVILISH SANDWICHES

(Yield: 5 dozen finger sandwiches)

1 (3-ounce) cream cheese, softened
1 (4 1/4-ounce) can deviled ham
1/2 (16-ounce) can whole berry cranberry sauce
2 loaves (1-pound 4-ounce size) whole wheat or white bread, crusts removed

In a small bowl, beat cream cheese until light and fluffy. Stir in deviled ham and cranberry sauce. Cover and chill overnight. Spread on bread next day.

SHRIMP SPREAD

(Yield: 3 dozen finger sandwiches - Make ahead)

- **2 (6-ounce) cans shrimp, well drained and diced**
- **$1/2$ cup butter or margarine, softened**
- **1 (8-ounce) cream cheese, softened**
- **$1/2$ cup mayonnaise**
- **1 tablespoon Worcestershire sauce**
- **$1/2$ cup onion, finely chopped**
- **$1/2$ cup celery, finely chopped**
- **2 tablespoons lemon juice**
- **2 loaves (1-pound size) whole wheat or white bread, crusts removed**

Mix well and chill overnight. Spread on bread for sandwiches.

NOTE: *To use this as an appetizer, place in bowl with spreaders, surrounded by crackers.*

TORTILLA WRAPS

- **1 (10 per pack) package large, round, flour tortillas**
- **2 (8-ounce) cream cheese, softened**
- **1 ($6\frac{1}{2}$-ounce) jar green olives, drained and chopped**
- **1 (15-ounce) can black beans, drained and mashed**
- **$1/2$ cup green onion, finely chopped**
- **$1/2$ teaspoon chili powder**

Divide tortillas, five to a bundle. Mix one cream cheese with olives. Spread on five of the tortillas and roll up tightly. Seal at edge with water. Wrap in plastic wrap and store overnight in refrigerator. Slice the roll into $1/4$ inch sections when ready to serve.

Mix second cream cheese with black beans, onion and chili powder. Spread on remaining five tortillas. Follow preparation instructions for first five wraps.

NOTE: *When cutting the rolls, do not serve the ends. They are not attractive, but still taste good! Put in plastic bag and eat later.*

SAUSAGE CHEESE BALLS

(Yield: 170 small balls)

3 cups biscuit baking mix
1 pound ground hot sausage, uncooked
2 cups sharp Cheddar cheese, grated

Mix all ingredients together. Refrigerate overnight. Roll into small balls and bake at 350° for 30 minutes. Cool. May be made months ahead, frozen and heated in low oven before serving.

BROCCOLI CORNBREAD MINIATURE MUFFINS

(Yield: 4 dozen)

2 tablespoons margarine, melted
1 (8½-ounce) box prepared cornbread mix
4 eggs, beaten
1 cup sharp grated cheese
1 small onion, chopped
1 (10-ounce) package frozen chopped broccoli, cooked 5 minutes and drained

Use 4 miniature muffin tins (12 per pan). Spray with vegetable cooking spray. Pour a few drops of melted margarine into each of the 48 muffins wells. Mix all the ingredients together and drop by teaspoon full into muffin tins. Fill greased muffin tins one-half full and bake at 350° for 15 minutes.

***NOTE:** To prepare and serve with a dinner meal, use ½ cup margarine. Melt in a square (9x9-inch) baking pan and spoon ingredients into pan. Bake at 400° for 40 minutes.When partially cooled, cut into squares. Or place in large individual muffin tins (12).*

RECIPES

Cheese Straws . . . . .Recipe on page 51

Party Mix . . . . .Recipe on page 29

FRANCES'S SPICED PECANS

1 cup sugar
½ teaspoon cinnamon
¼ cup milk
2 teaspoons water
½ teaspoon vanilla
2 cups pecan halves

Mix sugar and cinnamon together in saucepan. Add milk and water. Boil, stirring constantly, until a few drops form a soft ball in cold water. Add vanilla and remove from stove. Place pecans in pan and stir until mixture coats and hardens. Pour on wax paper and break apart. Store in covered container. Prepare in advance.

CREAM CHEESE COOKIES

(Yield: 6 dozen)

1 cup butter or margarine, softened
1 (3-ounce) cream cheese, softened
1 cup sugar
1 egg yolk
2½ cups flour
1 teaspoon vanilla
candied cherries or pecan halves

Cream butter and cream cheese; slowly add sugar, beating until fluffy. Beat in egg yolk. Add flour and vanilla; mix well Chill dough at least an hour. Shape dough into 1-inch balls; place on greased cookie sheets. Gently press a cherry or pecan half into each cookie. Bake at 325° for 12-15 minutes.

SAND TARTS

(Yield: 4-5 dozen)

1 cup butter or margarine, softened
3 tablespoons powdered sugar
3 tablespoons water
1 teaspoon vanilla
2 cups flour
1 cup chopped pecans
powdered sugar

Cream butter and powdered sugar together. Add other ingredients Mix well. Roll into small crescent shapes. Place on ungreased cookie sheets. Bake 350° for 20 minutes. After cool, roll in powdered sugar.

HONEY'S PEANUT BUTTER COOKIES

(Yield: 6 dozen)

1 cup vegetable shortening
2 cups sugar
1 cup creamy peanut butter
2 eggs, beaten
3 cups flour
1 teaspoon salt
2 teaspoons baking soda
2 teaspoons vanilla

Cream shortening and sugar. Add peanut butter, stir, add eggs. Sift flour, salt and soda together and blend into other ingredients. Add vanilla and mix well. Roll into balls, place on cookie sheets sprayed with vegetable cooking spray. Mash balls with salad fork (criss-cross). Bake at 350° for 20 minutes. Best made days ahead.

PECAN TARTS

(Yield: 2 dozen)

CRUST
1 (3-ounce) cream cheese softened
½ cup butter, softened
1 cup sifted four

FILLING
1 egg
¾ cup brown sugar
1 tablespoon soft butter
1 teaspoon vanilla
dash of salt
⅔ cup chopped nuts

For crust blend cheese and butter together and stir in flour. Chill for one hour. Shape dough into 2 dozen one-inch balls. Press balls on bottom and sides of small muffin tins. For filling, beat egg, sugar, butter, vanilla and salt until smooth. Add nuts. Fill cups. Bake at 325° for 25 minutes.

SPICY APPLESAUCE CAKE

(One pan)

1/3 cup oil
1 (18.25-ounce) box spice cake mix
2 eggs
1 (16-ounce) jar applesauce
powdered sugar

Preheat oven to 350°. Pour oil into a 13x9x2-inch pan; tilt pan until oil covers bottom. Combine cake mix, eggs and applesauce in pan. Stir with fork until blended (about 2 minutes). Bake 35-45 minutes. Sprinkle cooled cake with powdered sugar. Cut into squares to serve.

QUICK STREUSEL COFFEE BARS

(Yield: 25 bars)

1/2 cup margarine or butter, softened
1/2 cup sugar
1 egg, beaten
1 teaspoon vanilla
1 cup flour, sifted

TOPPING
1/3 cup sugar
1 teaspoon cinnamon
1 cup chopped pecans

Cream butter and 1/2 cup sugar in large mixer bowl. Add egg and vanilla. Mix well. Blend in flour. Spread in well greased 11x8x1-inch pan. For topping, combine 1/3 cup sugar with cinnamon, mix well and sprinkle over surface of batter; then sprinkle nuts over top. Press down lightly with hand, so streusel won't fall off when removing from pan. Bake at 350° for 25 -30 minutes.While warm cut into 2x1-inch bars. Freezes well.

PLUM CAKE

2 cups sugar
1 cup cooking oil
3 eggs
2 cups self-rising flour
2 (4-ounce) jars baby food plums
1 teaspoon cloves
1 teaspoon cinnamon
1 teaspoon vanilla
GLAZE
lemon juice
1½ cups powdered sugar

Mix all ingredients together in one bowl. Beat until smooth. Pour into greased and floured fluted tube pan. Bake at 325° for one hour. Stick center of cake with a clean broom straw and if it comes out clean it is done.

GLAZE: Mix small amount of lemon juice with 1½ cups of powdered sugar until smooth; thin to consistency required to pour over warm cake.

COFFEE PUNCH

(Yield: 50-60 servings)

16 cups slightly sweetened, strong coffee
8 cups milk
1 gallon vanilla ice cream

Let coffee cool. Add milk and chopped up ice cream. Serve in punch bowl.

(Yield: 25-30 servings)

12 cups slightly sweetened, strong coffee
6 cups milk
½ gallon vanilla ice cream

Let coffee cool. Add milk and chopped up ice cream. Serve in punch bowl.

Chapter 4

Family Dinner Parties at Thanksgiving and Christmas

Rice?
What to prepare?
Roast?
Potatoes?
Ham?
???
???
Happy Anniversary
Happy Anniversary
POTATOES

Chapter 4

Family Dinners at Thanksgiving and Christmas

MENU

Cranberry-Lime Salad
Assorted Olive, Relish and Pickle Tray
Cranberry Sauce
Squash Casserole
Green Beans
Spinach AuGratin
Macaroni and Cheese
Sweet Potato Casserole
Honey's Oven Roasted Turkey
Dressing
Holiday Muffins
Pecan Pie
No Crust Coconut Pie

Aren't family get-togethers wonderful? Nothing can top the special moments when our families have gathered around the dining room table for a joyous Thanksgiving or Christmas feast. I have been blessed by experiencing this every year. Even when I am the one that is preparing the food, it is a happy and exciting time.

The possibilities are limitless with table decorations for these two holidays. I always use my fine china, crystal, sterling silver flatwear, napkin ring holders, candlesticks with lighted candles, and I make place cards. Children enjoy these special touches as much as the adults.

Add a small favor at each place setting and this will help make the dinner more memorable. There were so many used when I was growing up, but one in particular stands out in my mind. Honey took a large red gum drop and pushed a white life-saver mint into the side for a handle, and placed a small green candle in the top, which she lit. This was not only pretty, easy to make but a lot of fun to have sitting on your bread and butter plate. When the candle burned down it extinguished itself in the gum drop. After the meal we would eat the drop and mint. That was a real treat!

The menu for these two holidays is the same, due to the popularity of the food with my family members. Although, there is a variation in the muffins and dressing. (This is noted in the recipes.) The selection of dishes has something to please every age and taste bud. All the food can be prepared in advance and keeps you out of the kitchen, so you may enjoy visiting with your family. I hope these will help you have an easier and happy holiday. The recipes are listed below.

CRANBERRY-LIME SALAD

(Yield: 12 half-cup servings)

2 (3-ounce) packages lime-flavored gelatin
4 cups boiling water
1 (6-ounce) can frozen limeade concentrate
2 cups uncooked cranberries
2 cups celery, diced
lettuce
sour cream

Dissolve gelatin in boiling water. Add frozen limeade and stir until dissolved. Refrigerate until syrupy. Cut cranberries into three pieces each. When gelatin has thickened, stir in cranberries and celery. Spoon into individual molds or a large mold and chill until set. Unmold on a bed of lettuce and garnish with sour cream. Make several days ahead.

PLANTATION SQUASH

3 pounds yellow squash, washed and cut up
1/2 medium onion, chopped
1/2 cup Italian bread crumbs
2 eggs, beaten
1/2 cup margarine or butter, melted
1 tablespoon sugar
1 teaspoon salt
1/2 teaspoon black pepper

Cook squash and onion together, until tender. Drain thoroughly, then mash. Add all ingredients except 1/2 of the butter. Mix together and pour into a greased, 2-quart baking dish. Spread remaining butter over top of ingredients and sprinkle with additional bread crumbs. Bake uncovered at 375° for one hour.

NOTE: May be made several days ahead, before the holiday, and kept in the refrigerator, covered. Take lid off one hour before baking and let the dish come to room temperature.

RECIPES

Green Beans . . . . .Recipe on page 18

Spinach AuGratin . . . . .Recipe on page 37

Sour Cream Biscuits . . . . .Recipe on page 30

No Crust Coconut Pie . . . . .Recipe on page 31

HONEY'S OVEN ROASTED TURKEY

1 (12-14 pound) turkey (frozen or fresh)
1 bottle of liquid smoke (comes in one size)
3 cups water
½ teaspoon salt
¼ teaspoon pepper
heavy duty aluminum foil for roaster lid, if needed

When using a frozen turkey, take it out of your freezer in plenty of time to thaw before making your preparations to bake. Reach in the neck cavity and you will find a bag of giblets (neck, gizzard and heart). Wash these and place them in water, with salt and pepper. Boil covered for 30 - 40 minutes. When finished cooking set the pot aside and save this broth to make your dressing.

Wash the turkey inside and out. Place it in a roasting pan or aluminum container large enough to hold the turkey. Shake the bottle of liquid smoke and pour over the entire turkey. While it is marinating, prepare your dressing to stuff inside the turkey. After the dressing is made and the bird is stuffed, make sure your roaster pan lid will fit properly. If not, make a cover with heavy duty aluminum foil.

Honey (my mother) taught me how to roast a turkey by letting it cook all night. My daughter and daughter in-law use this method also and really enjoy the freedom of hassle on the day of Thanksgiving or Christmas. All three of us are very happy that Honey taught us this easy procedure.

Preheat your oven to 500° and generously sprinkle salt over the turkey. Pour about an inch of water in your roaster, around the turkey, and secure the lid. Place the bird in the oven at 10 p.m. and bake for 30 minutes. Then reduce the heat to 275° and bake all night. At 7 a.m., or whenever you awaken, check the turkey. I usually have to use a baster and an empty saucepan and draw the excess liquid out and place it in the pan. Save this to heat and pour over the turkey slices when dishing up the plates for the dinner. This is called au jus, which is the broth from the turkey. After removing the roasting pan from the oven, keep the lid on until time to serve.

We always eat our main meal at noon,on these holidays, and it is amazing that the turkey stays warm till then. Of course, when you heat the au jus and ladle over the meat slices, the turkey is piping hot again. This baking method can still be used even if you aren't eating at the noon hour. All you need to do is figure the hours the turkey needs to bake and allow yourself the 30 minutes to start the baking in the 500 degree oven. This procedure is flawless and produces a mouth watering turkey.

DRESSING

1/2 cup onion, chopped
2/3 cup celery, chopped
1 cup butter or margarine
1 teaspoon salt
1/2 teaspoon pepper
1 teaspoon poultry seasoning
2 quarts (8 cups) bread crumbs (torn up bread slices)
1 1/2 to 2 cups broth

Cook onion and celery in butter over low heat until onion is soft but not browned, stirring occasionally. Meanwhile blend seasonings with bread crumbs. Add onion,celery and butter and mix. Pour the broth gradually over surface, stirring lightly. Add more seasoning as desired and more broth if the dressing is too dry. You are ready to stuff the turkey!

VARIATIONS:

Cornbread dressing: Add 4 cups cornbread, crumbled, then 4 cups of bread crumbs.

Oyster dressing: Cook 1 pint oysters in the oyster liquid until edges curl. Add to bread with seasoning. Include oyster liquid as part of the liquid in dressing. Chop oysters if they are large.

Chestnut dressing: Add 1 cup chopped chestnuts.

NOTE: When stuffing the turkey, if you have some dressing left over; place it in a greased baking dish. Cover and bake 350° for 30 minutes.

MACARONI AND CHEESE

1 cup macaroni
$1\frac{1}{2}$ cups sharp cheese, grated
1 egg, beaten
$\frac{2}{3}$ cup milk
salt and pepper

Cook and drain macaroni. Put in layers in casserole with one cup cheese. Mix egg, milk and seasonings and pour over macaroni. Top with remaining cheese. Bake at 375° until brown, approximately 20-25 minutes.

NOTE: Make days ahead and store in the refrigerator, covered, until day to bake. Uncover and warm to room temperature.

SWEET POTATO CASSEROLE

2 (13-ounce) cans of sweet potatoes, drained and mashed
1 cup white sugar
2 eggs, beaten
$\frac{1}{2}$ cup milk
2 teaspoons vanilla
$\frac{1}{2}$ cup butter or margarine, softened
$\frac{1}{2}$ teaspoon nutmeg
$\frac{1}{2}$ teaspoon cinnamon
2 cups miniature marshmallows

Mix all ingredients together, except marshmallows. Pour into a 2-quart greased baking dish and cover top with marshmallows. Bake 350° (uncovered) for 20-25 minutes.

NOTE: Make days ahead and store in the refrigerator, covered, until day to bake. Uncover and warm to room temperature.

HOLIDAY MUFFINS

(Yield: $1\frac{1}{2}$ dozen)

2 cups flour
3 teaspoons baking powder
3 tablespoons sugar
$\frac{1}{2}$ teaspoon salt
1 egg, well beaten
1 cup milk
3 tablespoons shortening, melted
$\frac{3}{4}$ cup cherries or blueberries, drained and chopped

Sift dry ingredients together. Combine egg, milk, and melted shortening. Add this to dry ingredients, together with fruit, and stir until just mixed. Fill greased muffin pans two-thirds full and bake at 425° for 20-30 minutes.

NOTE: Use blueberries at Thanksgiving and cherries at Christmas.

PECAN PIE

(Yield: 1 (9-inch) pie)

1/4 cup butter, melted
3 tablespoons flour
1 (1-pound) box light brown sugar
6 tablespoons milk
3 eggs
2 tablespoons vinegar
1 1/2 teaspoon vanilla
1 cup chopped pecans
1 unbaked 9-inch pie shell

Set aside melted butter to cool. Mix flour and sugar together. Add milk and eggs; beat well. Stir in vinegar and vanilla. Add melted butter and nuts; pour into unbaked pie shell. Bake at 300° for about 1 hour.

Notes

Chapter 5

40th Anniversary Dinner Party for Parents

Rice?
What to prepare?
Roast?
Potatoes?
Ham?
???
???
?
Happy Anniversary
Happy Anniversary
POTATOES

Chapter 5

40th Anniversary Dinner Party for Parents

MENU

Social Hour

Fruit Punch
Zesty Bacon Dip with Raw Vegetables
Smoked Oyster Delights
Party Mix

Dinner

Tomato Aspic
Assorted Pickles and Olives
Yellow Rice and Corn Casserole
Green Beans
Chicken and Broccoli Crepés
Quick Yeast Rolls
Anniversary Sheet Cake (purchased)

What a blessing to experience your parents having been married 40 years, and host a special dinner in their honor! After their casual 25th anniversary celebration, I thought Honey and Daddy deserved an outstanding dinner party to enjoy with their relatives and friends. That is exactly what I gave them and everyone had a great time. Especially me!

I followed the preparations, as outlined earlier in this book (see pages 9 -11). Therefore the entire party was easy and enjoyable.

Honey displayed her wedding dress at the party and it was the topic of much conversation during the event. I am proud to still have it today.

If you are fortunate to have parents or relatives that are celebrating an outstanding anniversary, I recommend you honor them with a similar event. Recipes are listed below.

♥♥♥♥♥♥♥♥♥♥♥♥♥♥♥♥♥♥♥

FRUIT PUNCH

(Yield: 25 servings)

2 (46-ounce) cans of apple juice, chilled
2 (46-ounce) cans of pineapple juice, chilled
1 (2-liter) bottle lemon-lime flavored carbonated beverage, chilled

Pour 2 cups of apple juice into a pitcher and add 2 cups pineapple juice, stir and pour into a 1 quart mold and freeze. The day before the party, run hot water on the back side of the mold, to remove the frozen juices. Wrap the frozen mold in foil and return to freezer. A few minutes before the party begins, pour the fruit juices and carbonated beverage in a punch bowl and stir until blended. Place the frozen juice mold on the top of the punch and serve. When making punch use some of the liquids (non-carbonated) to make cubes or molds, instead of ice cubes, so your punch isn't watery and diluted. You may add a few strawberries in the bottom of the mold, to give color.

ZESTY BACON DIP

1 (8-ounce) sour cream
1 (8-ounce) cream cheese, softened
4 slices bacon, cooked and crumbled
1 tablespoon chopped green onion
1 tablespoon dried parsley, may use fresh
1 tablespoon horseradish
1 tablespoon diced pimentos

Mix sour cream and cream cheese until well blended. Add all other ingredients, mix and chill overnight. Serve with crackers or raw vegetables.

SMOKED OYSTER DELIGHTS

(Yield: 2 dozen)

1 (4.75-ounce) jar jumbo green olives, drained
2 (3.7-ounce) cans petite smoked oysters, drained

Remove pimento from olives and stuff with petite oyster. Cover and refrigerate until ready to serve. Best to prepare a day ahead.

Party Mix . . . . .Recipe on page 29

TOMATO ASPIC

(Yield: 6-8 servings)

2 envelopes unflavored gelatin
1¾ cups tomato juice, divided
¼ teaspoon salt
½ teaspoon sugar
½ teaspoon Worcestershire sauce
⅛ teaspoon hot pepper sauce
2 tablespoons lemon juice

Sprinkle gelatin on 1/2 cup of the tomato juice to soften. Place over low heat and stir until gelatin is dissolved. Remove from heat and stir in remaining 1 1/4 cups tomato juice, add seasonings. Pour into a two cup mold or individual molds. Chill until firm. Overnight is best. Unmold on serving plate. Garnish aspic with salad greens and black olives.

YELLOW RICE AND CORN CASSEROLE

1 (5-ounce) bag yellow rice
1 (11-ounce) whole kernel corn, drained
¼ cup margarine, softened
1 (10¾-ounce) can cream of celery soup
1 cup grated Cheddar cheese

Cook rice as directed. Mix all ingredients together, except cheese, and place in greased 9-inch square pan. Top with cheese. Bake at 350° for 20-25 minutes, uncovered.

***NOTE:** Make days ahead and store in the refrigerator, covered, until day to bake. Uncover and warm to room temperature.*

Green Beans . . . . .Recipe on page 18

BASIC CREPÉS
(Yield: 14 crepés)

1 cup all-purpose flour
1½ cups milk
2 eggs
1 tablespoon cooking oil
¼ teaspoon salt

In a bowl combine flour, milk, eggs, oil and salt; beat with a rotary beater until blended. Heat a lightly greased 6-inch skillet. Remove from heat; spoon in about 2 tablespoons batter. Lift and tilt skillet to spread batter evenly. Return to heat; brown on one side only. Place finished crepe on paper towels. Repeat with remaining batter to make 14 crepés, greasing skillet occasionally. After crepés have cooled, place waxed paper between them. Make a stack (they are thin) and cover to store in refrigerator until assembling.

NOTE: Good idea to make several days ahead.

CHICKEN AND BROCCOLI CREPÉS
(Yield: 7 servings, 2 crepés each)

6 tablespoons butter or margarine
6 tablespoons flour
dash salt
3 cups milk
½ cup shredded sharp cheese
¼ cup cooking white wine
1 (2½-ounce) jar sliced mushrooms
1 (10-ounce) package frozen chopped broccoli, cooked and drained
2 cups finely chopped cooked chicken
14 basic crepés

FOR SAUCE

In a medium saucepan melt butter. Blend in flour and salt. Add milk all at once. Cook, stirring constantly, until thickened and bubbly. Stir in cheese and wine until cheese melts. Remove ½ cup of the sauce; set aside. Stir mushrooms into remaining sauce.

CHICKEN AND BROCCOLI CREPÉS
(continued)

FOR FILLING

Cook broccoli according to package directions and drain. Combine broccoli, chicken and the 1/2 cup reserved sauce.

TO ASSEMBLE

Spread 1/4 cup filling over unbrowned side of crepe, leaving 1/4 inch rim around edge. Roll up crepe. Place seam side down in greased 3-quart baking dish. Repeat with remaining crepés. Drizzle sauce over crepés. At this point, you may cover and refrigerate overnight. Remove cover and let dish come to room temperature before placing in a 300° oven. Heat until bubbly. Approximately 15-20 minutes.

RECIPES

Quick Yeast Rolls . . . . .Recipe on page 38

Anniversary Sheet Cake . . . . .purchased

Notes

Chapter 6

Wine and Cheese Parties

Rice?
What to prepare?
Roast?
Potatoes?
Ham?
???
???
Happy Anniversary
Happy Anniversary
POTATOES

Chapter 6

Wine and Cheese Parties

MENU POSSIBILITIES:

Salty

Cocktail Oyster Crackers

Barbecued Peanuts

Party Mix

Cheese Straws

Frances's Spiced Pecans

Dips

Smoked Oyster Dip

Dill Dip

Chili Cheese Dip

Parmesan Cheese Dip

Bacon Dip

Zesty Bacon Dip,

Clam Dip

Artichoke-Water Chestnut Dip

Barbecue Dip

Spinach Dip

Assorted Crackers and Corn Chips.

— Continued —

MENU POSSIBILITIES CONTINUED:

Spreads

Honey's Corned Beef Salad

Shrimp Spread

Cheese Ball

Pineapple Spread

Fresh Crab Spread

Salmon Log

Hot Artichoke Spread

Assorted Crackers and Corn Chips

Pick-Ups

Smoked Oyster Delights

Jill's Crab Meltaways

Deviled Eggs

Seafood Tartlets

Cucumber Delights

Sausage Cheese Balls

Tortillas Wraps

Dill Pickle Appetizers

Variety of Bulk Cheeses, cut into one-inch cubes (furnish toothpicks)

Tray of Fresh Fruits

Sweets

No-Bake Rum Balls

Orange Balls

Lemon Squares

Double Chocolate Brownies

Do you like cheese? If so, this party is for you! Now that you have handled so many different types of parties, up to this chapter, a wine and cheese party will be a "piece of cake". Whether your invitation list is large or small you will find this type of party one of the easiest to give. Why do I think so? Your food set-up is buffet style, the hors d'oeuvres are all finger foods, cooking may be done weeks ahead and it is economical.

You will notice I have given you a menu selection of thirty-four recipes. Those are enough for about five parties. Of course, you may purchase many canapes, already prepared, in the frozen section of your stores. They are tempting to use but are not as delicious as the homemade foods, and they cost more. So enjoy preparing the ones I have listed. You will be glad you did and your guests will be impressed.

If you are planning on more than twenty-five people I would suggest you set up two food stations. The dining and breakfast rooms are great to use. Always have your wine in a separate room so you won't have too many people in one area. Your den or great room would be perfect for your beverages.

When I am counting on forty or more guests, I fix three punch bowls full of different drinks. I prepare a white wine spritzer for one, which is four 10-ounce bottles of sparkling water and four cups of white wine. Chill this and pour into the bowl, floating fresh mint on the top for color. In another bowl I make a sangria punch. This is made with orange, cranberry, lemon juices and red wine. The proportion of the liquids is up to each hostess. I float thin slices of lemons, oranges and bananas on the punch. In the third bowl I furnish Cranberry Sparkle Punch (recipe on page 46).

After you complete your plans for decorations and all the other preliminaries, keep in mind that there are a lot of different containers to use when serving your food. I mentioned a large group of vessels to be used for flowers (Chapter 2, Casual Dinner Party for 8, pages 21-28) and now I would like to suggest some different ideas for serving bowls. Use a round loaf of bread, red or white cabbage, half of a pineapple, cantaloupe, small watermelon, grapefruit, or avocado, which have their centers scooped out. These are great for the dips. Your finger pick-ups will look good when using your typical platters, plates and trays, whether made of glass, china, silver, copper or pottery. For crackers think about using different sizes of baskets, decorative wooden boxes, vegetable serving bowls and fruit bowls. An empty shoe box spray-painted a color to match your décor, and lined with cloth napkins, is great for a large quantity of crackers. Put your thinking cap on and be creative and invent your own containers.

When finalizing your plans don't forget to establish your garnishes for each serving tray. The most standard garnish is parsley. Don't leave kale, fruits and flowers off your "ideas" list.

Your wine and cheese party will be very successful, and I am sure you will be ready to give them more often. I know your friends will be delighted if you do! Recipes listed below.

RECIPES

SALTY

Cocktail Oyster Crackers . . . . . . .Recipe on page 35

Barbequed Peanuts . . . . .Recipe on page 44

Party Mix . . . . .Recipe on page 29

Cheese Straws . . . . .Recipe on page 51

Frances's Spiced Pecans . . . . .Recipe on page 65

DIPS

CLAM DIP

1 (8-ounce) sour cream
1 (8-ounce) cottage cheese
1 (3.3-ounce) jar minced clams, drained
1 (2-ounce) jar pimentos, drained and finely chopped
2 tablespoons onion, finely chopped
1 tablespoon parsley flakes
½ teaspoon Worcestershire sauce
½ teaspoon salt
¼ teaspoon cayenne pepper
½ teaspoon lemon juice
1 tablespoon mayonnaise

Cream all ingredients together and if too stiff, add a little more mayonnaise. Cover, chill overnight. Serve with crackers.

ARTICHOKE-WATER CHESTNUT DIP

1 (8½-ounce) can artichokes, drained and chopped
1 (5-ounce) can water chestnuts, drained and chopped
½ cup mayonnaise
1 (1-ounce) package powdered buttermilk Ranch salad dressing mix

Day before the event, mix all ingredients together. Cover and store in refrigerator until ready to serve. Use corn chips as servers.

BARBEQUE DIP

1 (8-ounce) cream cheese softened
1/2 cup hickory-flavored barbeque sauce
1/2 cup finely chopped green onion

Mix well, cover and store in refrigerator until time to serve. Serve with bacon flavored crackers. Best made ahead.

SPINACH DIP

(Make at last minute.)

1 (10-ounce) package frozen chopped spinach, cooked and drained
3 cups (one-inch cubes) Jalapeno pepper cheese
corn chips

While spinach is hot add cheese cubes and stir. Cover, place in microwave oven and heat until cheese completely melts (approximately 2 minutes). Stir and reheat if needed. Serve immediately and use large corn chips as servers.

SPREADS

Honey's Corned Beef Salad . . . . . .Recipe on page 62

Shrimp Spread . . . . .Recipe on page 63

Cheese Ball . . . . .Recipe on page 35

PINEAPPLE SPREAD

1 (8-ounce) can crushed pineapple, drained
1 cup sugar
1 tablespoon mayonnaise
½ cup crushed pecans
2 (8-ounce) cream cheese, softened

Boil pineapple in sugar, drain. Add remaining ingredients and stir well. Cover, chill overnight. Serve with crackers and spreaders.

NOTE: My favorite serving container for this recipe is a fresh pineapple cut in half, leaving the top intact. Scoop out the center, and place the spread in the pineapple shell.

FRESH CRAB SPREAD

3 (8-ounce) cream cheese, softened
1 (12-ounce) bottle chili sauce
1 pound fresh lump crabmeat

Use a 9-inch or 10-inch round glass dish. Place the cheese in bottom, pour chili sauce over cheese and top with crab. Serve with crackers and spreaders. Assemble at the last minute.

SALMON LOG

1 (14.5-ounce) can salmon, drained and flaked
1 (8-ounce) cream cheese, softened
1 tablespoon lemon juice
2 teaspoons grated onion
1 teaspoon prepared horseradish
½ teaspoon salt
¼ teaspoon liquid smoke
½ cup pecans, chopped
3 tablespoons fresh parsley, chopped fine

Combine all ingredients together, except parsley and pecans. Shape into a log (8x2-inches) and roll in the pecans and parsley. Wrap in waxed paper and store in the refrigerator (days ahead) until ready to serve. Furnish crackers and spreaders.

HOT ARTICHOKE SPREAD

1 (8-ounce) marinated artichoke hearts, drained and cut up
1 cup mayonnaise
1 cup parmesan cheese
1 tablespoon garlic salt

Mix well and cover; store in refrigerator until ready to bake. Bring to room temperature and bake at 350° for 10 minutes. Leave in baking dish and have crackers and spreaders next to dish.

PICK-UPS

Smoked Oyster Delights . . . . .Recipe on page 83

Jill's Crab Meltaways . . . . .Recipe on page 29

Deviled Eggs . . . . .Recipe on page 45

Seafood Tartlets . . . . .Recipe on page 52

Cucumber Delights . . . . .Recipe on page 52

Sausage Cheese Balls . . . . .Recipe on page 64

Tortilla Wraps . . . . .Recipe on page 63

Dill Pickle Appetizers . . . . .Recipe on page 45

SWEETS

NO-BAKE RUM BALLS

(Yield: 6 dozen)

1 (16-ounce) can creamy vanilla frosting
3 cups graham cracker crumbs
1 cup firmly packed ground walnuts
1/4 cup (2 one-ounce) bottles rum flavoring
powdered sugar

In large mixing bowl combine all ingredients except powdered sugar. Stir well until blended. Shape into balls, using a teaspoon of mixture for each ball. Roll each ball in powdered sugar. Store in tightly covered jar. The older they are, the better!

ORANGE BALLS

(Yields 6 dozen)

1 (12-ounce) package vanilla wafers, crush to fine crumbs
1 pound box powdered sugar
1/2 cup margarine, softened
1 (6-ounce) can frozen orange juice
1 cup finely chopped pecans
1 (3.5-ounce) can flaked coconut

Mix all ingredients (except coconut) and form into small balls. Roll in coconut and store in airtight container in refrigerator until served.

RECIPES

Lemon Squares . . . . Recipe on page 48

Double Chocolate Brownies . . . . . Recipe on page 48

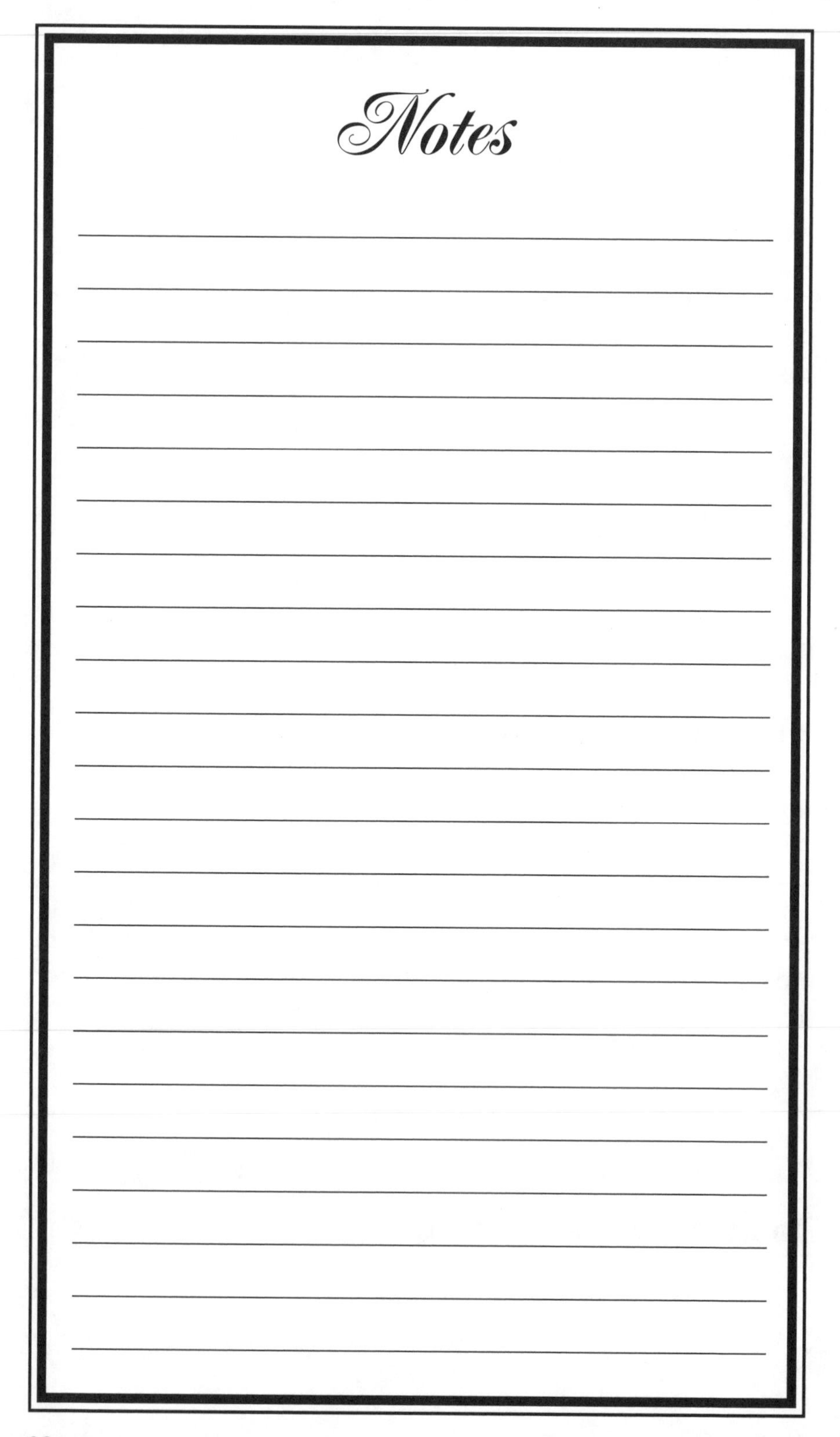
Notes

Chapter 7

Vegetarian Dinner Parties

Rice?
What to prepare?
Roast?
Potatoes?
Ham?
???
???
Happy Anniversary
Happy Anniversary
POTATOES

Chapter 7

Vegetarian Dinner Party

MENU

Social Hour

Sesame Party Mix (purchased)
with Assorted Nuts

Pineapple Pickups

Potpourri Pile

Fruit Punch

Dinner

Three Vegetable Casserole

Broccoli Rice Casserole

Marinated Vegetables

Yellow Rice and Corn Casserole

No-Bake Rum Balls

Orange Balls

Have you ever experienced a very difficult challenge involving hosting a party? Mine can top yours! When I volunteered to host a buffet dinner party for the Mobile Symphony Board of Directors and spouses, along with our visiting Conductor, I never dreamed what would happen.

After I went through all the steps of preparations, purchased the food (for 35 people) and started pre-cooking, I learned the Conductor was a vegetarian–not just meat but all dairy products.

At first I thought I would go on with my original plans and prepare the Conductor a single plate of vegetarian dishes, while the other guests had "normal" food. My love for a challenge won out and I made a new menu for the entire party. This required a lot of research.

I was "teased" by several of the guests when they heard it was going to be vegetarian all the way. They said they would stop at a fast food store and purchase a hamburger before arriving. Much to their surprise,the guests loved all the dishes and didn't miss the meat, cheese, eggs and milk.

All the recipes that I used are listed at the end of this section. Try them and surprise your guests!

PINEAPPLE PICKUPS

1 (20-ounce) can pineapple chunks
1¼ cups sugar
¾ cup vinegar
dash of salt
6 to 8 whole cloves
1 (4-inch) stick cinnamon

A day ahead or so, drain syrup from pineapple chunks. To ¾ cup syrup add vinegar, sugar, salt, cloves and cinnamon. Heat 10 minutes. Add pineapple chunks. Bring to boil. Refrigerate until time to serve. To serve, drain pineapple chunks and place cold fruit in shallow bowl with decorative picks.

POTPOURRI PILE

1 (6-ounce) can ripe, pitted, black olives, drained and chopped
1 (5-ounce) can green chilies, drained and chopped
2 medium sized ripe tomatoes, chopped
½ teaspoon wine vinegar
dash hot pepper sauce
1 tablespoon olive oil
2 or 3 green onions, chopped
dash garlic

Mix and chill. Serve with large corn chips.

LEMON-LIME FRUIT PUNCH

(Yield: 50 servings)

2 cups sugar
2 cups water
1 (46-ounce) can apricot nectar
1 (46-ounce) can unsweetened pineapple juice
1½ cups lemon juice
1 (6-ounce) can frozen orange juice, mixed according to directions on can
2 (2-liter) bottles lemon-lime flavored carbonated beverage, chilled

Combine sugar and water; heat until dissolved. Cool and chill. Add other juices. Chill until ready to serve. Make ice cubes (put a cherry in each) out of fruit juices. Gently combine juices with carbonated beverage in punch bowl. Float ice cubes on top.

THREE VEGETABLE CASSEROLE

(Adapted for non-dairy users)

2 (10-ounce) packages, frozen broccoli, cooked according to directions, and drained (save juice)
2 (10-ounce) packages, frozen brussel sprouts, cooked according to directions, and drained (save juice)
2 (10-ounce) packages, frozen cauliflower, cooked according to directions, and drained (save juice)
1 (2-ounce) box onion soup mix (2 envelopes)
toasted bread crumbs

WHITE SAUCE
Juice from cooked vegetables
1 tablespoon cornstarch
½ cup fresh mushrooms, chopped

Prepare two cups of white sauce from the juice from the cooked vegetables, cornstarch and the mushrooms. Cook until thickened. Mix vegetables with white sauce and onion soup mix. Place in greased 3-quart baking dish. Top with crumbs. Cover and bake at 325° for 25 minutes.

BROCCOLI RICE CASSEROLE

2 cups cooked instant rice
2 (10-ounce) boxes, frozen broccoli, cooked according to directions and drained, (save juice)
1 (10 ¾-ounce) can cream of chicken soup, undiluted
1 (15-ounce) jar processed cheese sauce

OPTIONAL
WHITE SAUCE
Juice from cooked broccoli
1 tablespoon cornstarch

Mix ingredients together and put in 2-quart casserole dish which has been sprayed with vegetable cooking spray. Sprinkle with paprika for color. Cover and bake at 350° for 25 minutes.

OPTIONAL: *To adapt recipe for guests that do not eat dairy products substitute White Sauce for the soup and cheese. Prepare White Sauce from the juice from the cooked broccoli and cornstarch. Cook until thickened.*

MARINATED VEGETABLES

(Yield: 12 servings)

1 1/2 cups vegetable oil
1 cup cider vinegar
1 tablespoon sugar
2-3 teaspoons dried dill weed
1 teaspoon salt
1 teaspoon pepper
1 pound fresh broccoli, washed and chopped
1 head cauliflower, washed and chopped
5 yellow squash, washed and chopped
5 carrots, scrapped and sliced thin
6 medium sized fresh mushrooms, diced

Combine first six ingredients in a jar. Cover tightly, shake vigorously. Add vegetables to marinade and cover. Refrigerate 24 hours. Occasionally shake to distribute marinade among the vegetables. Drain before putting in serving container.

YELLOW RICE AND CORN CASSEROLE

(Adapted for non-dairy users)

1 (5-ounce) bag yellow rice
1 (11-ounce) can whole kernel corn, drained (save juice)
1/4 cup margarine, softened
1 (2.8-ounce) can French fried onion rings

WHITE SAUCE
Juice from corn
1 tablespoon cornstarch
1/2 cup fresh celery, chopped

Cook rice as directed and set aside. Prepare white sauce from the juice reserved from the can of corn, cornstarch and celery. Cook until thickened. Spray a 2-quart baking dish with vegetable cooking spray. Mix rice, corn, margarine and white sauce together. Place mixture in dish and top with onion rings. Bake uncovered at 350° for 20-25 minutes.

RECIPES

No-Bake Rum Balls . . . . .Recipe on page 97

Orange Balls . . . . .Recipe on page 97

Notes

Chapter 8

Cooking "Mass" Meals for an Elderly Person

Rice?
?
What to prepare?
Roast?
Potatoes?
Ham?
???
???
Happy Anniversary
Happy Anniversary
POTATOES

Chapter 8

Cooking "Mass" Meals for an Elderly Person

MENU

6 Different Entrées

Roast Beef with Carrots,
Onions, Rice and Green Beans

Baked Fresh Turkey Breast with
Dressing, Squash and Mixed Vegetables

Meat Loaf with Macaroni,
Turnips and Cauliflower

Baked Chicken with Rice,
Canned Beets and Spinach

Baked Fish
(purchased from the grocery store)

Chinese Chicken Chow-Mein
(purchased from a restaurant)

This chapter has nothing to do with entertaining but information in this chapter will help someone who needs to be a care-giver for an elderly person or parent. Besides, the recipes are perfect to use for dinner parties.

Honey (my precious mother) was not nursing home material, but after my daddy died she lost the desire to cook for herself. She wouldn't eat and as a result lost 45 pounds. Her mind was fine but her body became fragile. I moved her into an apartment complex near my home, and God gave me the vision to help Honey. She was the one who taught me the art of cooking so I decided to cook her meals. Therefore she started eating my precooked dinners and it was as though she had cooked them herself.

Honey could not order "Meals-on-Wheels" due to a low salt, low cholesterol and ulcer diet. When I started cooking and freezing meals I would cook enough for one month. I worked out a six entrée menu which she rotated. They were roast beef, baked turkey, meat loaf, baked chicken, and baked fish and Chinese food.

I purchased the baked fish in the frozen food section of my grocery store. The Chinese food was chicken chow-mein and I ordered it from a local restaurant, making sure they held the monosodium glutamate.

After selecting the dinner she wanted to eat, Honey would take it out of her freezer an hour early. This would allow it to thaw before heating the meal in her conventional oven.

I worked out an assembly line system, using aluminum roll pans (9x6x1-inches) and covering them in aluminum foil after filling the containers. I used a black marker to write the name of the entrée on top. I kept the bulk of the dinners in my home (I used a large upright freezer) with a tally sheet on the outside of the door. I would check my list once a month and when a certain entrée was getting low I knew it was time to start cooking again.

Honey had a tally sheet also and would mark it after she had eaten the dinner. I would restock her small refrigerator/freezer every two weeks. I had a real meals-on-wheels from daughter to mother.

Can you believe I did this for fourteen years? Until Honey died, this was a true labor of love!

The cooking section of our local newspaper wrote a feature story on my concept. They printed the recipes and all the details about the logistics of my fete. Many people called and thanked me for sharing my story. It helped them to take care of their loved ones in similar situations.

I was asked many times, during the fourteen years, if I disliked cooking so much for my mother. I can honestly say that at times I became tired, but then I would remember how much my mother loved me and was the one who taught me how to cook, and all the tired feelings would go away. I have no regrets and if I had the opportunity I would do it again. I received a blessing from having the chance to show Honey how much I loved her and appreciated all she had done for me through the earlier years of my life. The recipes are listed on the following pages.

ROAST BEEF

(Yield: 20-22 servings)

5 to 6 pound rump roast
corn oil margarine
2 cups water
2 pounds fresh carrots, scraped and cut into 2-inch lengths
6 medium white onions, peeled and sliced
low sodium salt

Preheat oven to 500°. In large dutch oven on top of the stove, brown roast in small amount of corn oil margarine. Add water, carrots and onions; sprinkle salt. Cook, covered, in oven for 30 minutes. Reduce heat to 350° and continue cooking for 3 hours. Check after 2 hours and add water if necessary.

While the roast is baking, cook two cups of regular rice and four pounds of fresh green beans. (recipe for green beans on page 18).

When roast has cooled, remove vegetables and place in a large bowl. Place roast on platter and peel fat off bottom of roast before slicing into serving pieces.

ASSEMBLY

Spray 20 aluminum roll pans (9x6x1-inch) with vegetable cooking spray and assemble the roast, carrots, onions, green beans and rice. Pour au jus over the roast, rice and carrots. Cover the pans with foil and mark with a black marker "Roast" on each, before freezing.

BAKED FRESH TURKEY BREAST

(Yield: 20 servings)

1 (7 pound) fresh turkey breast
salt substitute
garlic powder
2 cups water

Wash turkey breast and place in Dutch oven. Sprinkle with salt substitute and garlic powder. Add water and cover. Place in preheated 500° oven for 30 minutes. Reduce heat to 325° and bake for three additional hours. When turkey breast is done, cool. Remove skin and slice into serving pieces. Use juice from pan to baste the slices. While the turkey bakes prepare two boxes of stuffing mix. Use a low sodium brand that has calcium (no MSG - monosodium glutamate) as a preservative.

COOKED SQUASH

(Yield: 20 servings)

3 (1-pound) bags frozen (no salt added) squash
water
3 tablespoons sugar
2 teaspoons salt substitute
1 medium onion, chopped fine
1 (1-pound) plastic squeeze bottle of corn oil margarine

In a 3-quart baking dish, add squash, water, sugar, salt substitute and onion. Mix well; cover dish with clear plastic wrap. Cook on high in microwave oven for 20 minutes. Turn dish around, add more water if needed. Recover and cook 20 minutes longer. Drain, pour into large bowl.

MIXED VEGETABLES

(Yield: 20 servings)

Cook three (1-pound) bags of frozen mixed vegetables (broccoli, carrots, cauliflower) the same way, but omit the sugar. Drain and set aside.

ASSEMBLY

Spray 20 aluminum foil pans (9x6x1-inch) with vegetable cooking spray and assemble the turkey, dressing and vegetables. Squeeze the margarine over all. Cover the pans with foil and mark with a black marker "Turkey" on each before freezing.

MEAT LOAF

(Yield: 18-20 servings)

3 pounds lean ground beef (sirloin)
3/4 cup egg substitute
1 tablespoon salt substitute
1 tablespoon onion powder
1 tablespoon garlic powder
1 tablespoon Worcestershire sauce
1 tablespoon parsley flakes
1/2 cup low salt catsup
12 "no salt" saltine crackers, broken into small pieces

In large mixing bow, break up ground beef with fork; add remaining ingredients. Mix well and place in 2-quart baking dish which has been sprayed with vegetable cooking spray. Mash down with a fork and pat with hands until it is smooth on top, leaving a small space around sides and ends. Pour additional catsup over entire top. Bake in 350° preheated oven (uncovered) for one hour. Cool and slice into serving pieces.

While meat loaf bakes; prepare 1 (12 ounce) bag shell macaroni according to package directions. When done, drain, stir in 100% corn oil squeeze margarine, salt substitute and grated low-fat mozzarella cheese. Set aside.

In 2-quart baking dish place three 1-pound bags frozen turnips (no salt added). Add water, 3 tablespoons sugar, salt substitute and chopped medium sized onion. Cover with plastic wrap and cook in microwave oven 25 minutes, turn, add more water if needed, stir, recover and cook 25 minutes longer. Drain and set aside.

Cook three 1-pound bags frozen cauliflower (no salt added) the same way but omit sugar. Reduce the cooking time to 15 minutes, turn, stir and cook 10 minutes longer, adding water if necessary. Drain; set aside.

ASSEMBLY

Spray 20 aluminum roll pans (9x6x1-inch) with vegetable cooking spray and assemble the meat loaf, macaroni, turnips and cauliflower. Squeeze corn oil margarine over all except the meat loaf. Cover the pans with foil and mark with a black marker "Meat Loaf" on each, before freezing.

BAKED CHICKEN

(Yield: 16 servings)

2 cups uncooked rice
2 (2-ounce) boxes onion soup mix (2 envelopes per box)
16 skinless, boneless chicken breasts
2 (12-ounce) cans low fat evaporated milk
1 (1-pound) plastic squeeze bottle corn oil margarine

Cook rice and set aside. Spray two 2-quart baking dishes with vegetable cooking spray. Divide rice, placing half in each dish. Open one box soup mix and put one envelope of mix in a small bowl; mix well. Using a spoon, sprinkle this over rice in one dish. After the chicken breasts are washed, place 8 on top of rice/soup mixture in one dish. Pour one can of evaporated milk over the chicken. Pour squeeze margarine over tops of chicken breast. Take second envelope of soup mix (from first box) and mix and spoon over chicken.

Assemble second baking dish in the same manner. Cover both dishes with foil and bake in preheated 425° oven for 1/2 hour. Reduce heat to 225° and bake 1 hour. After baking is completed, set aside.

ASSEMBLY

Open four (15-ounce) cans of beets (no salt added) and four (27-ounce) cans of spinach. Drain both. Assemble dinners with same procedure as other entrées: spray 16 roll pans, place chicken in each, with rice, beets and spinach. Squeeze margarine over beets and spinach. Cover with foil and mark "Chicken" on each, before freezing.

Notes

Chapter 9

Stud Party

Rice?
What to prepare?
?
Roast?
Potatoes?
Ham?
???
???
Happy Anniversary
Happy Anniversary
POTATOES

Chapter 9

Stud Party

MENU

Dill Pickle Appetizers

Party Mix

Cheese Straws

Honey's Corned Beef Salad
with Assorted Crackers

Cream Cheese with Pineapple on
Cranberry/Raisin Bread Sandwiches

Orange Balls

Peanut Butter Cookies

No-Bake Rum Balls

Naughty, naughty, I know what you are thinking! Sorry to disillusion you, it was a "sneak preview party" for our new home under construction. The house was nothing but studs, sub-flooring and a temporary roof overhead, which set the stage for a different and fun party!

With no electricity installed, we were fortunate to have the house far enough along to have our guests in early June, before the hot summer weather arrived. The hours of the very, very, casual party were from 5 to 7 p.m.

Our only daughter, Laura, in North Alabama, hosted a similar party and that is where I came up with the idea. She used newspapers on her food and beverage tables, but I used white, plastic disposable cloths.

I placed a 6-foot folding table in our future dining room and used a basket full of silk summer flowers on the table. The beverages (assorted soft drinks and wine) were on a separate card table in the same room. Paper plates, napkins and cups were used, and the guests helped themselves to the refreshments.

Prior to the party I purchased white poster boards and wrote the name of each room "to be". I thumb tacked each to a stud denoting the room. Our friends wandered around, upstairs and downstairs, viewing our new home and visiting with mutual friends.

Two of my close girlfriends were stationed in the kitchen at a card table with two folding chairs, trash bags, paper towels, jugs of water (plumbing wasn't installed) and kept the food table filled. I prepared the food ahead of time, and brought it to our construction site in ice chests.

I didn't have a large variety of food but I had a sizable amount of each item. I used clear plastic serving trays and servers. The menu used is listed at the beginning of this chapter. The page numbers are listed below for your easy reference in finding the recipes.

I greeted our guests (approximately 95) standing in the framed-in window, with no window installed, near our open doorway. That was a surprise greeting! Everyone seemed to have a great time, and I know I did!

I do believe this was the easiest party I have ever given since I didn't have to clean the house before or after the event. The ants enjoyed the left over crumbs!

RECIPES

Dill Pickle Appetizers . . . . .Recipe on page 45

Party Mix . . . . .Recipe on page 29

Cheese Straws . . . . .Recipe on page 51

Honey's Corned Beef Salad . . . . . .Recipe on page 62

Cream Cheese with Pineapple on Cranberry/Raisin Bread Sandwiches . . . . .Recipe on page 61

Orange Balls . . . . .Recipe on page 97

Honey's Peanut Butter Cookies . . .Recipe on page 66

No-Bake Rum Balls . . . . .Recipe on page 97

Notes

Chapter 10

Open House Party

Rice?
?
What to prepare?
Roast?
Potatoes?
Ham?
???
???
POTATOES
Happy Anniversary
Happy Anniversary

Chapter 10

Open House Party

MENU

Finger Sandwiches
Sausage Cheese Balls
Broccoli Cornbread Miniature Muffins
Tortilla Wraps
Cheese Straws
Party Mix
Frances's Spiced Pecans
Cranberry Sparkle Punch
Magic Bars
Linda's Easy Cookies
Bourbon Balls

Following our "Stud Party", Chapter 9, my husband and I hosted an open house. Our friends were eager to see our home completely finished, and this was accomplished several months after we moved in.

I followed the same procedure as described in Chapter 6, "Wine and Cheese Party" (pages 91-92), and prepared all the food in advance.

Our invitation list was composed of several hundred people. To avoid a "mob scene" I divided my list in half. When I had the invitations printed I used the hours of 3 to 5 p.m. on one half and 6 to 8 p.m. on the others.

Open house parties are a perfect way to entertain a large group of people. The buffet set-up and finger foods make it easy to feed this large number, especially when you place your refreshments in different rooms.

In addition to inviting your friends and relatives to view a new home, the holiday seasons are a wonderful time for an open house. Of course, the opening of a new business is another reason to host this style party. Whatever the need, enjoy accomplishing this event! Recipes are listed below.

RECIPES

18 Recipes from Chapter 3, Coffee Parties . . . . .Recipes from pages 61 to 68

Cranberry Sparkle Punch . . . . . .Recipe on page 46

Spiked Punch . . . . .Recipe on page 46

MAGIC BARS

½ cup butter
1½ cups graham cracker crumbs
1 cup pecans, chopped
1 cup chocolate chips
1⅓ cups coconut
1 (14-ounce) can sweetened condensed milk

Melt butter in 13x9x2-inch pan. Sprinkle graham cracker crumbs on butter, then add nuts, chocolate chips and coconut. Pour sweetened condensed milk over all. Bake at 350° for 25 minutes. Cool and cut into bars.

LINDA'S EASY COOKIES

(Leannah's daughter-in-law)

(Yield: 3 dozen medium or 4 dozen small cookies)

1 (18.25-ounce) yellow cake mix
2 eggs
1/2 cup cooking oil
1 (6-ounce) bag chocolate chips - OR -
1 (8-ounce) bag of round candy-coated chocolate pieces

Mix all ingredients by hand. By teaspoon full, roll into balls. Bake on cookie sheets sprayed with vegetable cooking spray. Bake at 350° for 5-6 minutes.

BOURBON BALLS

(Yield: 50 balls)

1 1/2 cups sifted powdered sugar
1/3 cup bourbon
1/4 cup light corn syrup - OR - honey
2 1/2 cups crushed vanilla wafers (about 75)
1 cup coarsely chopped pecans
1 tablespoon unsweetened cocoa powder

Mix 1 cup of the sugar, bourbon and corn syrup in bowl. Add wafers and nuts. Stir until evenly moistened. Pinch walnut-sized piece from mixture and roll firmly between palms to form a ball. Repeat with rest of mixture. Sift remaining 1/2 cup sugar with cocoa onto wax paper. Roll balls in cocoa mixture to coat evenly. Store in airtight container with wax paper between layers. Substitute 1/3 cup orange juice or espresso for the bourbon if you wish. Best when made weeks in advance.

Notes

Chapter 11

Bridal or Baby Shower

Rice?
?
What to prepare?
Roast?
Potatoes?
Ham?
???
???
Happy Anniversary
Happy Anniversary
POTATOES

Chapter 11

Bridal or Baby Shower

MENU

Party Mix
Frances's Spice Pecans
Party Mints (purchased)
Cheese Straws
Heart Shaped (Open-Faced) Sandwiches
"Calla Lily" Sandwiches
Egg Salad Finger Sandwiches
Orange Balls
Double Chocolate Brownies
Lemon Squares
Fruit Punch

What a wonderful time to host a party for a bride elect or mother-to-be! Make your plans in advance, as outlined in "Preparations for Entertaining" (pages 9-11).

My menu suggestions, listed above, are a perfect blend to suit all palates. The food selection is your decision but I want to mention that I only use the "calla lily" sandwiches for wedding showers. They look like a bride-elect, but not a mother-to-be.

For the baby shower I substitute a star shaped (open faced) sandwich. If you don't own a cutter that shape, or unable to purchase one, use a small round cutter. Prepare Devilish Spread (page 62) and use on these sandwiches. The devil's food gives them a pinkish look. I tint the open-faced, heart-shaped, sandwiches a light blue (cream cheese spread) for the baby shower and this gives you a "pink" and "blue" décor.

I have found with previous showers the ladies attending do not eat an abundance of food, due to their excitement. Keep this in mind when you are purchasing and preparing the food.

When making your pre-arrangements don't forget to order a corsage for the honoree, as well as your gift for the bride elect or mother-to-be.

Picture in your mind a beautifully set table at a reception with lots of pretty flowers and silver serving pieces. That is what you should aim for, when planning the party. If you don't have silver items to use for serving trays it will look just as nice to use china or glass trays. Refer to "Casual Dinner Party for 8", Chapter 2, page 21-28, and read my suggestions for making flower arrangements throughout your home and the party table. Be sure to purchase extra flower bouquets at the grocery store for garnishes on your food trays.

Since the table is set for buffet serving it is all right to use a large flower arrangement. For the wedding showers I have given I used a variety of things for the flower container: a striped hat box (laying the lid at an angle against the side of the box), silver footed bowl, large straw hat with brim (hat turned upside down), large straw basket and several china tea pots. If you are going to use a hat box, basket or straw hat, be sure you put something in it to hold water for the flowers.

I am fortunate to own a large, footed mirrored tray. I place this in the middle of the table and set the flower container on top. If you do not have one of these, go to a glass store that sells mirrors and have one cut in a square or the size of a short runner. The top to my wedding cake (small bride and groom dolls) is on display in my home, under a glass doom. I place that on the mirrored tray next to the flower arrangement. This makes a special touch for the wedding shower.

The containers that I have used for baby showers have been a large silver footed bowl, crystal bowl or a child's doll buggy.

If you don't own a buggy, borrow one or buy it. You can usually find these at a thrift or dollar store. Mine is spray painted white. I place a glass bowl in the bottom to hold the water for arranging the greenery and flowers.

On the mirrored tray, around the base of the flowers, I sprinkle aluminum (cut out) small confetti. These come in different colors and shapes of a bride and groom, wedding bells, and hearts, as well as baby bottles, rattles and shoes. You may purchase these at a party supply store or stationary store. When the party is over store them in a small zip-top plastic bag and save them for your next shower. They really add the perfect look to your pretty table.

We are fortunate to be able to buy nice looking clear (small) disposable, plastic plates for the guests to use as they are serving themselves. They are made with a scroll design on the bottom of the plate and are attractive. When you are at the party supply store purchase small napkins with the wedding or baby motif on them, to be used with the plates.

Once everything is under control with the food selection, decorations and table set up, it is time to establish a place for the shower itself. Select a large room and make sure you have enough chairs for everyone that is planning on attending. You also need a large table (or use one that is in the room but clear it off) for the guests to put their gifts for the honoree. Remember to place a trash can, note pad and pen, scissors and tape, next to the gift table, so that the guest of honor may post the items as she opens them. She needs to ask someone to help her with the opening so all the gifts may be properly identified. It is a good idea to have an additional table in the room to display the presents as they are opened.

As soon as the guests arrive have them serve themselves to the refreshments. Playing games isn't popular today so the ladies can enjoy eating, visiting and taking photographs. After the first hour have the honoree start opening her gifts.

If you have never given a shower you have missed a treat! Start looking for one to give, and you will be so happy when you do. I guarantee it! Recipes listed below.

RECIPES

Party Mix .Recipe on page 29

Frances's Spiced Pecans . . . . .Recipe on page 65

Party Mints . . . . .purchased

Cheese Straws . . . . .Recipe on page 51

HEART-SHAPED (OPEN-FACED) SANDWICHES

(Yield: 38 sandwiches)

2 loaves (1 pound 4 ounces) white bread, crust trimmed, Cut into heart shapes with cutter (approximately 3x3½ inches) Keep in a zip-top plastic bag as you cut the bread so it doesn't dry out. Prepare day ahead and store in refrigerator.
1 (8-ounce) tub of cream cheese with pineapple
few drops of red food coloring
waxed paper

Place cream cheese in small bowl and blend the food coloring to make a pretty pink color. Store in refrigerator. Right before the party, spread the sandwiches and arrange on a tray. Garnish with parsley. Cover with waxed paper until guests arrive.

"CALLA LILY" SANDWICHES

(Yield: 38 sandwiches)

2 loaves (1 pound 4 ounces) white bread, crust trimmed, Cut into round shapes with cutter (approximately 3x3 inches) Keep in a zip-top plastic bag as you cut the bread so it doesn't dry out. May use a plastic round lid from an empty peanut butter jar to cut the bread. Prepare day ahead and store in refrigerator.

1 (3-ounce) cream cheese, softened

2 tablespoons apricot preserves

1 (2.25-ounce) bag slivered almonds

3 drops yellow food coloring

38 green stems trimmed from parsley, used as garnish

Mix cream cheese with preserves the day before the party and store in refrigerator. Count 38 slivers of almonds; and seal the remaining almonds in a small zip-top plastic bag (mark date on bag) and keep in your freezer until the next party. Place the 3 drops of yellow food coloring in a small, shallow, bowl with a little water. Drop the 38 almond slivers in the water and stir until they turn bright yellow. Drain on paper towels and when dry, wrap them in clear plastic and save until you assemble the sandwiches the next day. The almonds are your stamens! Right before the party take your bread rounds and make (one at a time) your "Calla Lilies." Thinly spread the bottom half of the bread round with the cream cheese mixture (which is at room temperature) and fold the end over. You have a lily! Stick one tinted almond sliver inside the lily (leave enough sticking out to be seen.) Place lilies on platter (heading the same direction) and stick a parsley stem in the bottom of each for the lily stem. Pretty as a picture!

RECIPES

Egg Salad Finger Sandwiches . . . .Recipe on page 61

Orange Balls . . . . .Recipe on page 97

Double Chocolate Brownies . . . . .Recipe on page 48

Lemon Squares . . . . .Recipe on page 48

Fruit Punch . . . . .Recipe on page 82

Chapter 12

Wharf Party

Rice?
?
What to prepare?
Roast?
Potatoes?
Ham?
???
???
Happy Anniversary
Happy Anniversary
POTATOES

Chapter 12

Wharf Party

MENU

Cocktail Oyster Crackers

Party Mix

Smoked Oyster Dip
with Large Corn Chips

Shrimp Spread with Crackers

Salmon Log

Honey's Corned Beef Salad Sandwiches

Devilish Sandwiches

Cream Cheese with
Pineapple Sandwiches

Pecan Tarts

Cream Cheese Cookies

No-Bake Rum Balls

Talk about unusual, you wouldn't believe it! It was rare and not the "run of the mill" party, but it sure was a lot of fun! My husband purchased a new 30 foot sailboat. I decided to celebrate by inviting friends to the marina, where the boat was docked, to view it and have a party at the same time.

We invited a small group (10 couples) as we didn't want to overcrowd the "grown-up toy". Beverages were served on board with edibles on the wharf, adjacent to the vessel. Clever nautical invitations were mailed two weeks prior to the event, stressing shorts or slacks as the dress code.

All the food items were prepared in advance and transported to the marina in ice chests, as well as the ice and beverages. I placed two 6-foot folding tables on the wharf and used white plastic, disposable tablecloths. Large sea shells decorated the tables, and held the cloths down. I placed small plastic crabs and lobsters all around the tops of the tables to finish the decor. The food was served from sea shell shaped clear plastic trays and bowls. Red plastic plates and nautical designed napkins were available for the guests, along with plastic servers.

Again, no clean up, before or after the party. The seagulls enjoyed all the crumbs. Another easy party!

No wharf overlooking a river or lake? What about hosting an outdoor party to welcome a new horse (at the stables), a new motorcycle (at home on your deck) or a new camper (at a retreat)? Your possibilities are endless. Remember to be creative and just have fun! Recipes are listed on the following pages.

RECIPES

Notes

Chapter 13

Soup Sampling Party

Rice?
?
What to prepare?
Roast?
Potatoes?
Ham?
???
???
Happy Anniversary
Happy Anniversary
POTATOES

Chapter 13

Soup Sampling Party

MENU

Soups

Leannah's Vegetable Gumbo

Corn Chowder

Shrimp Soup

Artichoke Soup

Seafood Gumbo

Cream of Crab Soup

Wild Rice-Mushroom Soup

Lurline's Cheese Vegetable Soup

Breads

Broccoli Cornbread Miniature Muffins

Miniature Sour Cream Biscuits

Sweets

No-Bake Rum Balls

Orange Balls

Honey's Fruit Cake Cookies

Beverages

Fruit Punch

Spiked Fruit Punch

Have you attended a soup sampling party? Not only did I go to this style party but later hosted one. A good friend brought the idea from Oklahoma and was nice enough to permit me to utilize her idea. I changed the format of the party and used different soup recipes.

I chose the first part of December to host the soup sampling. My home was decorated in a Christmas motif and I selected red cards (5x7-inch) with dark green lettering for the invitations. These were mailed to a hundred ladies (post card rate) two weeks prior to the event. The invitation stated "drop by while shopping to sample soups and visit friends, before returning to the malls". The hours were between 11 a.m. to 2 p.m.

My dining room table and breakfast room table were used for the foods. My menu is listed at the beginning of this Chapter. Two punch bowls were on a table in my large den.

Most of the soups were prepared in advance and frozen. I thawed them in the refrigerator the day before the party. The muffins and biscuits, as well as the desserts, were cooked weeks ahead.

I borrowed several soup tureens and with my own I had four on each table. I placed trays under each bowl, to catch drippings and protect the table tops. A row of holly was arranged around the bases with different colored glass Christmas balls tucked away in the greenery. For the center of the tables I used extra tureens (one per table) with holly and additional ornaments. No cloths were used on the tables but red Christmas runners were placed under the center arrangements.

The muffins and biscuits were served from round crystal bowls (2 on each side of the tables).

Plastic Christmas punch cups, sterling silver teaspoons and paper Christmas napkins were furnished for the guests to serve themselves. Several of my friends loaned me their silver spoons and I was very careful to keep a list, so that I could return them to the rightful owners. The punch cups served as soup bowls for the sampling. I made place cards and set them in front of each tureen denoting the soup name.

Crystal serving trays held the desserts on sideboards in the dining room and breakfast room. The two large punch bowls were placed on a 6-foot folding table, in the den, covered with a Christmas table cloth. Plastic punch cups (with holly designs on the sides) and red and green napkins were placed next to the bowls of punch. White place cards denote the type of punch in each bowl.

All the ladies had a wonderful time going from room to room sampling the different soups and visiting with friends. I hired a lady to keep the soup tureens filled when needed, so I could mingle with my guests. Talk about compliments, I really received them!

I look forward to hosting this soup sampling party in the near future. Why don't you join me and give one also? Recipes listed on the following pages.

LEANNAH'S VEGETABLE GUMBO

(Yield: 40 cups- 2½ gallons)

4 cups water
1 tablespoon salt
2 teaspoons pepper
1 large onion, chopped
1 cup tomato catsup
¼ cup Worcestershire sauce
¼ cup dried parsley
2 (28-ounce) cans cut green beans, drained
2 (28-ounce) cans mixed vegetables, drain, dice carrots and potatoes
2 (15-ounce) cans English peas, drained
2 (1-pound 12-ounce) cans diced, peeled tomatoes, drained
1 cup uncooked rice
1 cup uncooked pasta (any shape, I use shells)

OPTION

3 cups leftover cooked chicken, turkey, or ham. Then I name it
"Vegetable Chicken Gumbo"
"Vegetable Turkey Gumbo"
"Vegetable Ham Gumbo"

Boil 4 cups water in 2 1/2 gallon (40 cups) pot with lid. Add salt, pepper, onion, catsup, Worcestershire sauce, and parsley. Stir, and add remaining ingredients. This is very thick. Add additional water until it reaches right below the top of the pot. Stir, cover, and resume boiling. After bringing to a rolling boil, stir, reduce heat to simmer, cover and cook for one hour. Remove lid every 20 minutes, stir and add water when it is below the "full" level continue cooking for an additional hour. Continue to check, stir, and add water. At the end of the second hour turn the stove off and let it sit the rest of the day. Then ladle into containers and freeze. When thawing to serve, do not add water. Soup should be thick.

CORN AND SAUSAGE CHOWDER

(Yield: 8 servings)

1 pound sausage
1 large onion, chopped
3 large potatoes, peeled and diced
2 teaspoons salt
$1/2$ teaspoon pepper
1 teaspoon basil
2 cups water
1 ($16 1/2$-ounce) can creamed corn
1 ($16 1/2$-ounce) can whole kernel corn, undrained
1 (12-ounce) can evaporated milk

Crumble sausage in skillet and brown. Drain off fat. Save 2 tablespoons of the fat. Put sausage and 2 tablespoons of the fat in deep sauce pan. Saute onion with the sausage. Add potatoes, salt, pepper, basil and water. Cover and simmer 15 minutes. Stir in the cream corn, whole corn with liquid and evaporated milk. Cover and heat **almost** to boiling.

SHRIMP SOUP

(Yield: 8 servings)

$2 1/2$ pounds shrimp, peeled
4 cups (1 quart) milk
1 pint cream
4 tablespoons butter
2 tablespoons flour
salt and pepper to taste
sherry to taste

Grate shrimp and add to milk. Place in top of double boiler and cook over hot water for $1/2$ hour. Remove from heat and add cream, butter, flour, salt and pepper. Stir well, add sherry just before serving because this improves the flavor.

ARTICHOKE SOUP

(Yield: 8 servings)

2 tablespoons onion, finely chopped
3 tablespoons butter
2 tablespoons flour
1½ cups chicken broth
2½ cups half and half
1 (16-ounce) can artichoke hearts, drained and diced
salt and cayenne pepper, to taste

Saute onion in butter for 5 minutes. Stir in flour and cook slowly for 2 minutes. Slowly add broth and half and half. Stir with whisk over low heat to thicken. Stir in artichokes and seasonings. Serve and enjoy.

SEAFOOD GUMBO

(Yield: 10 servings)

¼ pound butter
4 tablespoons flour
8 cups water
5 fresh tomatoes, chopped fine
2 pounds fresh okra, chopped
1 pound fresh crabmeat
1 pint raw oysters
2 pounds small, fresh raw shrimp, peeled
2 pounds fresh, boneless fish, cut into pieces
salt and pepper to taste
steamed white rice

Melt butter and add flour. Make a smooth paste and stir constantly over heat until it turns a rich brown, being careful not to burn it. Add water, tomatoes and okra. Cook slowly for one hour. Add crabmeat, oysters, shrimp and fish. Cook for 15 minutes, stir and add seasonings. Soup should be thick. Have bowl of steamed rice ready to spoon into bowls before adding gumbo.

CREAM OF CRAB SOUP

(Yield: 6 servings)

1 small onion, chopped
2 tablespoons butter
1 (8-ounce) can cream of potato soup
1 (8-ounce) can cream of celery soup
1 empty can full of water
1 empty can full of half and half
1 (5 - 7½ ounce) can crabmeat, drained
2 tablespoons dried parsley
salt and pepper to taste
¼ cup cooking sherry

In a large pan saute onion in melted butter. Add soups, water, half and half, crabmeat and parsley. Stir and add salt and pepper. Heat to boiling, stir and add sherry. Remove from heat and serve.

WILD RICE-MUSHROOM SOUP

(Yield: 6 servings)

3 tablespoons butter
1 medium onion, finely chopped
3 tablespoons flour
3 cups chicken broth
1 (4-ounce) can mushrooms, drained and chopped
2 cups cooked wild rice
1 cup half and half
½ teaspoon salt
dash pepper

Melt butter in saucepan, saute onion. Stir in flour and continue stirring over low heat, until flour is well mixed. Gradually add chicken broth, stirring constantly until thickened. Add remaining ingredients and heat slowly, stirring often.

LURLINE'S CHEESE VEGETABLE SOUP

(Yield: 4 quarts)

6 cups water
4 medium potatoes, peeled and cubed
1 medium onion, chopped
3 chicken bouillon cubes
1 (16-ounce) bag of mixed vegetables (broccoli, cauliflower and carrots)
1 pound processed cheese loaf, cut into small cubes
1 (10¾-ounce) can cream of chicken soup
pepper to taste
no salt

Boil water and add potatoes and onion, cook until almost done. Add bouillon cubes and mixed vegetables, continue cooking. After vegetables are cooked, add cheese and soup. Add pepper to taste, no salt. Stir until blended.

BEVERAGES

Cranberry Sparkle Punch . . . . . . .Recipe on page 46

Spiked Punch . . . . .Recipe on page 46

BREADS

Broccoli Cornbread Miniature Muffins . . . . .Recipe on page 64

Miniature Sour Cream Biscuits .Recipe on page 30

SWEETS

No-Bake Rum Balls . . . . .Recipe on page 97

Orange Balls . . . . .Recipe on page 97

HONEY'S FRUITCAKE COOKIES

(Yield: 4 dozen)

2½ cups flour
1 pound candied red cherries, chopped
½ pound candied red pineapple, chopped
½ pound candied green pineapple, chopped
4 cups chopped pecans
1 cup butter, softened
1 cup sugar
½ teaspoon salt
½ teaspoon ground cloves
½ teaspoon cinnamon
5 eggs
⅛ cup white cooking wine

Measure 1 ½ cups flour and mix fruit and pecans to coat, set aside. Cream butter and sugar. Sift in remaining flour (1 cup) and add spices. Mix with butter and sugar. Add eggs and wine, stir, add fruit and nuts, stir. Drop by teaspoonful on greased cookie sheets. Bake at 350° for 15 minutes.

Notes

Chapter 14

Vacation Home at the Beach Parties in the Carport

Rice?
What to prepare?
Roast?
?
Potatoes?
Ham?
???
???
Happy Anniversary
Happy Anniversary
POTATOES

Chapter 14

Vacation Home at the Beach
Parties in the Carport

MENU

Shaved Ham for
Build-Your-Own Sandwiches
(on potato rolls)

Lettuce Leaves, Mayonnaise, Mustard,
Relish, Tomatoes and Cheese Slices

Honey's Potato Salad

Leannah's Baked Beans

Chips

Hot Dogs

Honey's Peanut Butter Cookies

Double Chocolate Brownies

Linda's Easy Cookies

Assorted Beverages

Don't have a vacation home at the beach? This party can be used around a swimming pool, patio, neighborhood street party and many other gatherings.

While we owned our summer "get away" I took the opportunity each Memorial Day, Fourth of July and Labor Day to have parties.

We invited a large group of our friends and their children to come during the morning hours and spend the day. I never knew how many would attend or how long they would stay. I used an easy format with a buffet in the carport. I set up three 6-foot tables and placed the food and beverages out of the sun, sand and inclement weather.

This arrangement worked fine, as everyone could come and go, eating whenever they wanted to. They had the choice of swimming, walking on the beach, playing board games on blankets in our courtyard or just relaxing. The food stayed out all day and I could have fun too.

White plastic disposable cloths were used and large conk shells were placed on the tables with 8x10-inch American flags on dowel sticks, inserted in the shells. These served as anchors for the cloths. Dinner size red plastic plates were furnished with red, white and blue paper napkins and white plastic utensils. The table décor was certainly patriotic!

I purchased a 3 pound, fully cooked, half of a boneless ham and the butcher "shaved" it into thin slices. The ham was placed on a tray that was sitting on top of a larger container with ice, and covered with clear plastic wrap. I furnished potato rolls (precut) for the people to make their own sandwiches. A variety of condiments were placed next to the ham. Using plastic squeeze bottles of mayonnaise (18-ounce) and prepared mustard (16-ounce) helped keep spillage to a minimum.

The potato salad was served in the same manner as the ham. It was placed in a glass bowl on top of a larger bowl of ice, covered in clear plastic wrap.

I served Leannah's Baked Beans. To keep them warm all day I covered the container with aluminum foil and placed it on an electric warming tray.

The hot dogs were cooked inside, placed in heated buns and individually wrapped in aluminum foil. These were stored in an insulated cooler, alongside the food tables, and were ready for those who desired them. Tomato catsup (36-ounce) plastic squeeze bottle was sitting next to the other condiments. Chips were available in large clear plastic sea shell bowls, covered with clear plastic wrap.

The sweets were arranged on clear plastic fish shaped trays and covered with plastic wrap.

An additional ice chest held mixed beverages. The guests could help themselves to the food and drinks off and on during the day. Occasionally I would check and furnish refills as needed.

Our holidays at the beach were very special, and even more so with the presence of our friends and their families. Recipes listed on the following pages.

HONEY'S POTATO SALAD

(Serves 20)

10 eggs, hard boiled, peeled and separated. Put yolks in bowl and set aside. Finely chop whites.
10 potatoes, boil until done, drain, peel and dice
2 medium onions, finely chopped
4 ribs celery, washed and chopped
1 (10-ounce) jar sweet pickle relish, drained
2 cups mayonnaise
3/4 cup prepared mustard
2 tablespoons salt
1 teaspoon pepper
paprika

Mix all ingredients together (except the egg yolks and mustard). Mix egg yolks and mustard together in a separate bowl. Blend this into the potato mixture. If too stiff add additional mayonnaise. Taste and add more salt if desired. Cover and store in the refrigerator until served. Right before placing on the table, sprinkle with paprika for color. Best made a day ahead.

LEANNAH'S BAKED BEANS

(Yield: 20 servings)

2 (1 pound-7 ounce) cans pork and beans
1 1/2 cups light corn syrup
1/2 cup prepared mustard

Mix all ingredients together and heat at 350° for 30 minutes.

RECIPES

Honey's Peanut Butter Cookies . . Recipe on page 66

Double Chocolate Brownies . . . . . Recipe on page 48

Linda's Easy Cookies . . . . Recipe on page 127

Chapter 15

Breakfast or Brunch Parties

Rice?
What to prepare?
?
Roast?
Potatoes?
Ham?
???
???
Happy Anniversary
Happy Anniversary
POTATOES

Chapter 15

Breakfast or Brunch Parties

MENU

Hot Fruit Casserole
Garlic Cheese Grits
Sausage and Egg Casserole
Marylee's French Toast Casserole
Fried Bacon Slices
Sour Cream Biscuits
Assorted Jellies
Variety of Juices
Milk
Hot Tea
Coffee

Ever heard of Mardi Gras? Would it surprise you to learn that Mobile is the birthplace of Mardi Gras in the United States? Many balls are held during this time.

A long time ago I decided it would be enjoyable to invite our dance guests for breakfast, following our organization's ball. This was a buffet, in our home, and held at 1 a.m. Balloons and Mardi Gras dolls (jesters and clowns) decorated the food table and house. I prepared the food (except the bacon) several days prior to the breakfast and left it covered and heating in low ovens, while attending the ball.

The morning of the event I fried 4 pounds of bacon in an electric skillet, drained it, and left it *uncovered* in a 200° oven while the other foods warmed.

As soon as we reached our home, along with the eight guest couples, several of the ladies helped me place the food and beverages on the table.

This breakfast was so successful we continued it for many years (18 to be exact). For the second breakfast, after the dance, I planned on developing a new menu. Due to the insistence of our friends the food remained the same --- a tradition at the Holland's.

The recipes listed on the following pages are suitable for a brunch or any other party requiring breakfast foods.

HOT FRUIT CASSEROLE

(Yield: 12-15 servings)

1 (15-ounce) can mandarin oranges, drain and cut in half
1 (14-ounce) jar red apple rings, drain and cut into 2-inch size
2 (15-ounce) cans peaches, drain and cut into small sizes
1 (15-ounce) can pears, drain and cut into small chunks
2 (15¼-ounce) cans pineapple chunks, drained
1 (16-ounce) jar whole red cherries, drained
2 tablespoons flour
½ cup brown sugar
½ cup butter, melted
1 cup cooking sherry

Mix fruit together in a 3-quart greased baking dish. After mixing flour, sugar, butter and sherry, pour over fruit. Bake at 350° until liquid bubbles and fruit is hot. Approximately 35-40 minutes.

GARLIC CHEESE GRITS

(Yield: 8 servings)

1 cup grits, cook according to directions
½ cup butter, melted
1 (6-ounce) roll pasteurized processed cheese with garlic
2 eggs, beaten
½ cup milk

Mix grits, butter and cheese until blended. Add eggs and milk. Bake in greased 2-quart baking dish at 350° for 45 minutes.

SAUSAGE AND EGG CASSEROLE

(Make ahead and refrigerate overnight. Yield: 6-8 servings)

1 (1-pound) roll sausage, browned and drained
6 slices bread, broken into small pieces
6 eggs, beaten
2 cups milk
1 teaspoon salt
1/2 teaspoon white pepper
1 cup grated Cheddar cheese

Grease 9x12-inch baking dish and place all ingredients in dish, in order as listed above. Cheese on top. Cover, leave in refrigerator overnight. Uncover, warm to room temperature and bake at 350° for 45 minutes.

MARYLEE'S FRENCH TOAST CASSEROLE

(Make ahead and refrigerate overnight. Yield: 6-8 servings)

1 (1/2 pound) loaf French bread, cut into one inch slices
6 large eggs, beaten
3 cups milk
4 teaspoons sugar
3/4 teaspoons salt
1 tablespoon vanilla
2 tablespoons butter, cut into small pieces

Grease 9x13 inch baking dish and place bread in bottom of dish. Pour eggs, milk, sugar, salt, and vanilla (after mixing together) over bread. Dot with butter. Cover, refrigerate overnight. Bake, uncovered, after warmed to room temperature, at 350° for 55-60 minutes.

Sour Cream Biscuits . . . . .Recipe on page 30

Chapter 16

Bridge Parties

Rice?
?
What to prepare?
Roast?
Potatoes?
Ham?
???
???
Happy Anniversary
Happy Anniversary
Potatoes

Chapter 16

Bridge Parties

MENU

Ladies' Luncheon at Noon

Honey's Corned Beef Salad
on a Bed of Lettuce

Frozen Cranberry Salad

Broccoli Quiche

Orange Gelatin Salad

Henny Penny Pockets

Jill's Crab Meltaways

Melted Cheese-Olive Sandwiches

Tomato Aspic

Laura's Mock Chicken Cordon Bleu

Egg Salad on a Bed of Lettuce

Grandmother Leannah's Congealed Salad

Homemade Soups (8 different recipes)

Hot Crab Sandwich

Reuben Casserole

Broccoli Cornbread Miniature Muffins

Sour Cream Biscuits

Quick Nut Bread

Frozen Lemonade Pie

Frozen Chocolate Pie

Frozen Key Lime Pie

Ann's Buttermilk Pie

Lemon Squares

Chess Cake Squares

Couples' Desserts in the Evening

Frozen Lemonade Pie
Frozen Chocolate Pie
Frozen Key Lime Pie
Ann's Buttermilk Pie
Chess Cake Squares,
Ice Cream Dessert
Old Fashioned Pound Cake
Custard Pie
Caramel Sauce
Ozark Pudding

Don't play bridge? What about hearts, canasta, poker or pinochle? If you haven't invited friends over to join you in playing cards, give it a try. This is a good way to have fun and entertain at the same time.

Card playing not your "cup of tea"? Have friends over and use these recipes for a luncheon or dessert party.

Grandmother Leannah taught me the art of playing bridge when I was 11 years old. She was an avid player and held many ladies' bridge parties in her home. During the summer months I enjoyed helping her serve the guests.

For my ladies' bridge parties I prepare the food in advance and pre-set the table, in my dining room. Two dozen or more luncheon possibilities are listed at the beginning of this chapter.

I like to play bridge in a separate room. This saves time at the end of our meal and allows moving back into the playing area without stopping to clear the table. (Be sure you leave your flatwear soaking)

The guests arrive in my home at 10 a.m. and we play bridge for two hours. Snacks are on the bridge table or tables, and I serve soft drinks or coffee while we are playing. If I haven't had the opportunity to place the food on the table by the time we break for lunch, I ask someone to help me.

After completing the luncheon we are ready to return to the bridge table or tables, and resume playing. When the ladies are preparing to leave, I receive many compliments on the fun day.

Shortly after Lyman and I were married I added couples' bridge parties to our list of entertaining fetes. Both of us enjoy playing bridge and are fortunate to have several couples that take delight in this card game. Most of our couples' bridge functions are held in the evening.

When our guests arrive in our home at 7 p.m. we play bridge for two hours. I have snacks and soft drinks available while playing. The dessert is served around 9 p.m. with coffee, milk or water.

Upon completion of dessert we play bridge for several additional hours before our friends leave. Another successful party! Recipes are listed on the following pages.

Ladies' Luncheon at Noon

Honey's Corned Beef Salad . . . . .Recipe on page 62

FROZEN CRANBERRY SALAD

(Yield: 8 servings)

1 (16-ounce) can whole berry cranberry sauce
1 (8-ounce) can crushed pineapple, drained
1 teaspoon orange juice
1 (8-ounce) sour cream

Combine ingredients in a bowl; stir until blended. Pour mixture into 12 paper lined muffin cups. Freeze. Remove 15 minutes before serving and peel paper away. Place salads on lettuce.

Variation: *Pour mixture into a 8½ x 4½-inch loaf pan; cover, freeze until firm. Cut into 1 inch slices and serve on lettuce leaves.*

BROCCOLI QUICHE

1 deep dish pie shell, prepared
1 (8-ounce) package of broccoli buds, cook according to directions on package, drain
1 (8-ounce) shredded sharp cheese
4 eggs, beaten
2 cups milk
dash nutmeg

Mix broccoli and cheese; place in bottom of pie shell. Blend eggs, milk and nutmeg and pour over mixture in pie shell. Bake at 350° for 30-35 minutes until golden brown and mixture is firm.

ORANGE GELATIN SALAD

- 1 (6-ounce) orange gelatin
- 1 cup hot water
- 1 (8-ounce) can crushed pineapple, do not drain
- 1 (11-ounce) can mandarin oranges, drained and diced
- 1 cup chopped pecans
- 1 (3.5-ounce) flaked coconut
- 1 (8-ounce) sour cream

Combine gelatin and water in a 2-quart mold. Chill until syrupy. Add other ingredients. Return to refrigerator until firm, cut into desired sizes to serve. Make a day ahead.

HENNY PENNY POCKETS

(Yield: 5 servings)

- 1 (10-ounce) package refrigerated biscuits small amount of flour
- 1 (12.5-ounce) can chicken, drained
- 1/4 cup sour cream
- 1/4 cup shredded sharp cheese
- 1/8 teaspoon garlic powder
- dash pepper
- 1 large egg white, slightly beaten

Roll each biscuit (on a floured surface) into a 4 inch circle. Mix chicken, sour cream, cheese and seasonings. Spoon one tablespoon of chicken mixture onto one side of a biscuit. Brush water on edges of circle and fold over. Crimp edges with a fork. Brush with egg white. Place on a greased baking sheet. Bake at 400° for 8-10 minutes, until brown. Makes 10, serve 2 each.

Jill's Crab Meltaways . . . . .Recipe on page 29

MELTED CHEESE-OLIVE SANDWICHES

(Yield: 12 open-faced sandwiches)

2 cups shredded sharp cheese
1 (6-ounce) can black olives, drained and chopped
½ cup mayonnaise
1 tablespoon dried, chopped onion
1 package of split English muffins

Mix all ingredients together and spread on muffin halves. Bake at 350° for 15 minutes or until melted. Freezes well before baking.

Tomato Aspic . . . . .Recipe on page 83

LAURA'S MOCK CHICKEN CORDON BLEU

(Leannah's daughter, Laura)

(Yield: 8 servings)

8 chicken breasts, skinned and boned
salt to taste
1 (8-ounce) cream cheese
½ cup finely chopped green onion (use whole onion)
16 strips bacon

Cover chicken breasts with waxed paper and pound thin. Salt chicken. Cut cream cheese into 8 strips. Roll cheese in onion and place on chicken. Wrap chicken around cheese and go around chicken with one slice of bacon from top to bottom. Wrap other bacon slice around middle section so that the cheese is completely sealed inside. Place on broiler pan and broil 4 inches from the broiler. Cook 8-10 minutes on each side. Serve immediately.

NOTE: *This recipe may be prepared up to the point of broiling, one to two days ahead.*

RECIPES

Egg Salad on Bed of Lettuce . . . . .Recipe on page 61

Grandmother Leannah's Congealed Salad . . . . .Recipe on page 16

Homemade Soups . . . . .Recipes on pages 148-152

HOT CRAB SANDWICHES

(Yield: 6 sandwiches)

12 slices thin sliced bread, crusts removed and buttered with soft margarine (4 tablespoons)
1 (7½-ounce) can crabmeat, flaked and drained
½ pound Cheddar cheese, grated
4 eggs, beaten
3 cups whole milk
½ teaspoon salt

Place 6 slices bread, buttered side up, in a greased 13x9x2-inch baking dish. Spread crabmeat on the 6 slices of bread and cover with remaining bread. Sprinkle cheese over all. Combine eggs, milk and salt and pour over sandwiches. Bake at 325° for 50-60 minutes or until puffy and brown.

REUBEN CASSEROLE

(Yield: 4-6 servings)

1 (12-ounce) can corned beef, flaked
¼ cup Thousand Island dressing
1 (16-ounce) can sauerkraut, drained
1¾ cup Swiss cheese, grated
½ cup butter, melted
6 slices rye bread, cubed

Place corned beef in buttered 2-quart casserole. Spread on dressing and sauerkraut. Add grated cheese. Toss bread cubes with melted butter. Top casserole with bread cubes. Bake uncovered at 350° for 30 minutes or until hot and bubbly.

RECIPES

Broccoli Cornbread Miniature Muffins . . . . .Recipe on page 64

Sour Cream Biscuits . . . . .Recipe on page 30

QUICK NUT BREAD

(Yield: 2 loaves)

½ cup sugar
1 egg
1¼ cups milk
3 cups biscuit baking mix
1½ cups chopped pecans

Combine first four ingredients and beat hard for 30 seconds. Stir in nuts. Bake in 2 well greased (8½ x 4½ x 2½-inch) loaf pans at 350° for 45 minutes.

FROZEN LEMONADE PIE

(Yield: 2 recipes make 3 pies)

1 (14-ounce) can sweetened condensed milk
½ (12-ounce) can frozen lemonade, thawed, do not dilute, return other ½ can to freezer
1 (8-ounce) sour cream
1 (8-ounce) frozen, non-dairy, whipped topping, thawed
blue or red food coloring
1 (6-ounce) butter crust or graham cracker prepared pie shell
candied cake sprinkles

Mix milk and lemonade. Stir in sour cream and whipped topping. Add a few drops of blue food coloring if you want a blue pie (for men) or a few drops of red coloring to make a pink pie (for women). Pour into pie shell.

This recipe fills 1½ pie shells, so if you make the recipe twice, you have 3 pies. If you prefer, put the leftover filling from the first pie into the empty non-dairy whipped topping container, cover and freeze. Serve frozen in sherbet dishes and sprinkle cake sprinkles on top.

After you pour the pie mixture into the first pie shell, sprinkle cake sprinkles on top to decorate. Place pie in freezer and after hard, remove and lay the clear plastic lid, from the pie shell, on top to seal. Keep frozen until you cut and serve.

***NOTE:** Nice to double the recipe at first. These extra pies in the freezer make great gifts or ready to serve to guests. Stays fresh in freezer for 6 months or more.*

FROZEN CHOCOLATE PIE

(Yield: 2 recipes make 3 pies)

2 (7-ounce) milk chocolate bars, melted
1 (12-ounce) frozen, non-dairy, whipped topping, thawed
1 (6-ounce) chocolate crumb prepared pie shell
candied cake sprinkles

Melt chocolate over low heat, in large saucepan, stirring constantly. Blend in whipped topping until thoroughly mixed. Pour into pie shell.

This recipe fills $1^1/_2$ pie shells, so if you make the recipe twice, you have 3 pies. If you prefer, put the leftover filling from the first pie into the empty non-dairy whipped topping container, cover and freeze. Serve frozen in sherbet dishes and sprinkle cake sprinkles on top.

After you pour the pie mixture into the first pie shell, sprinkle cake sprinkles on top to decorate. Place pie in freezer and after hard, remove and lay the clear plastic lid, from the pie shell, on top to seal. Keep frozen until you cut and serve.

***NOTE:** Nice to double the recipe at first. These extra pies in the freezer make great gifts or ready to serve to guests. Stays fresh in freezer for 6 months or more.*

FROZEN KEY LIME PIE

(Yield: 2 recipes make 3 pies)

1 (14-ounce) can sweetened condensed milk
½ (12-ounce) can frozen lime juice, thawed, do not dilute, return other ½ can to freezer
1 (8-ounce) sour cream
1 (8-ounce) frozen, non-dairy, whipped topping, thawed
green food coloring
1 (6-ounce) chocolate crumb prepared pie shell
candied cake sprinkles

Mix milk and lime juice. Stir in sour cream and whipped topping. Add a few drops of green food coloring and stir. Make it the desired shade of green by adding more drops of coloring. Pour into pie shell.

This recipe fills 1½ pie shells, so if you make the recipe twice, you have 3 pies. If you prefer, put the leftover filling from the first pie into the empty non-dairy whipped topping container, cover, freeze. Serve frozen in sherbet dishes and sprinkle cake sprinkles on top.

After you pour the pie mixture into the first pie shell, sprinkle cake sprinkles on top to decorate. Place pie in freezer and after hard, remove and lay the clear plastic lid, from the pie shell, on top to seal. Keep frozen until you cut and serve.

NOTE: *Nice to double the recipe at first. These extra pies in the freezer make great gifts or ready to serve to guests. Stays fresh in freezer for 6 months or more.*

RECIPES

Ann's Buttermilk Pie . . . . .Recipe on page 55

Lemon Squares . . . . .Recipe on page 48

CHESS CAKE SQUARES

(Yields 24 squares)

1 cup butter, softened
1 (1-pound) box light brown sugar
½ cup granulated sugar
2 cups sifted flour
1 teaspoon baking powder
1 cup chopped pecans
1 teaspoon vanilla
powdered sugar

Mix butter and sugars. Add remaining ingredients, except powdered sugar. Pour in greased and floured 13x9x2-inch baking pan. Bake at 300° for 45 minutes. Cool for 10 minutes and sprinkle with powdered sugar. Cut in squares. Top with aerosol whipped dessert topping and a cherry.

Couples' Desserts in the Evening

RECIPES

Frozen Lemonade Pie
(tint one blue and one pink) . . . . .Recipe on page 176

Frozen Chocolate Pie . . . . .Recipe on page 177

Frozen Key Lime Pie . . . . .Recipe on page 178

Ann's Buttermilk Pie . . . . .Recipe on page 55

Chess Cake Squares . . . . .Recipe on page 179

ICE CREAM DESSERT

¾ cup butter, melted
1 (12-ounce) box vanilla wafer crumbs
½ cup chopped pecans
½ gallon vanilla ice cream

Pour butter over crumbs and nuts. Mix well. Put 1/2 of this mixture in a 3-quart dish. Cover with ice cream and sprinkle remainder of crumbs over top. Freeze. Cut into squares to serve and pour hot fudge sauce over dessert.

SAUCE
1 cup sugar
3 tablespoons cocoa
3 tablespoons flour
1 cup milk
1 teaspoon vanilla
4 tablespoons butter

Cook sugar, cocoa, flour and milk until thick, stirring constantly. Boil one minute. Add vanilla and butter after cooking. Store unused sauce (in glass jar) in refrigerator. Heat in microwave oven when needed.

OLD FASHIONED POUND CAKE

1 cup butter, softened
1⅔ cups sugar
5 eggs
2 cups flour, sifted, remeasured and sifted 5 additional times
1 teaspoon vanilla

Cream butter and sugar, continue mixing until sugar is no longer grainy. Add eggs one at a time, beating well after each addition. Continue beating until batter is fluffy. Add flour, mixing until well blended, and add vanilla. Pour into greased and floured fluted tube pan. Bake at 275° for 2 hours or until done.

CUSTARD PIE WITH CARAMEL SAUCE

4 eggs, slightly beaten
1/2 cup sugar
1/2 teaspoon salt
2 cups scalded milk
1 teaspoon vanilla
1/2 teaspoon nutmeg
9-inch prepared unbaked deep dish pie shell

Mix eggs, sugar and salt. Slowly add milk and vanilla mixing well. Pour into pie shell. Sprinkle with nutmeg. Bake on lower shelf of oven at 425°for 25-30 minutes, or until custard is firm. Drizzle caramel sauce over pie. See recipe for Carmel Sauce.

CARAMEL SAUCE

3/4 cups light brown sugar, firmly packed
1/3 cup light corn syrup
1/3 cup whipping cream
1/8 cup butter
dash of salt

Combine all ingredients in a small saucepan. Cook over medium heat, stirring constantly until the mixture is smooth and reaches boiling point. (Approximately 5 minutes.) Remove from stove and cool. Drizzle over slices of Custard Pie before serving. Store in refrigerator.

OZARK PUDDING

(Yield: 4-6 servings)

1 egg, slightly beaten
3/4 cup sugar
1 cup chopped apple
1/2 cup walnuts, chopped
3 tablespoons flour
1 1/2 teaspoons baking powder
dash of salt

Mix eggs and sugar, add apple and nuts. Mix well. Add the flour, baking powder and salt. Pour into greased 1-quart baking dish. Bake at 350° for 25 minutes. Serve warm or cold with whipped cream or ice cream on top.

INDEX

APPETIZERS

BEVERAGES

BREADS AND SANDWICHES

CAKES

COOKIES

DESSERTS

EGG AND CHEESE DISHES

FRUIT

MEAT

PIES

POULTRY

SALADS

SAUCES

SEAFOOD

SOUPS

VEGETABLES

EXTRA HELP

QUANTITIES TO SERVE 100 PEOPLE

Coffee	3 pounds	Baked Beans	5 gallons
Sugar	3 pounds	Beets	30 pounds
Cream	3 quarts	Cauliflower	18 pounds
Whipping Cream	4 pints	Cabbage for Slaw	20 pounds
Milk	6 gallons	Carrots	33 pounds
Fruit Cocktail	2 1/2 gallons	Bread	10 loaves
Fruit Juice	4 (6-lb.) cans	Rolls	200
Tomato Juice	4 (6-lb.) cans	Butter	3 pounds
Soup	5 gallons	Potato Salad	12 quarts
Oysters	18 quart	Fruit Salad	20 quart
Weiners	25 pounds	Vegetable Salad	20 quart
Meat Loaf	24 pounds	Lettuce	20 heads
Ham	40 pounds	Salad Dressing	3 quarts
Beef	40 pounds	Pies	18
Roast Pork	40 pounds	Cakes	8
Hamburger	30-36 pounds	Ice Cream	4 gallons
Chicken for Pie	40 pounds	Cheese	3 pounds
Potatoes	35 pounds	Olives	1 3/4 pounds
Scalloped Potatoes	5 gallons	Pickles	2 quarts
Vegetables	4 (6-lb.) cans	Nuts	3 pounds sorted

To serve 50 people, divide by 2

To serve 25 people, divide by 4

Special Thanks to...

Marylee K. Sund, *Crystal Lake, Illinois*

Michelle B. Wise, *Mobile, Alabama*

and Betty P. Ferguson, *Germantown, Tennessee*

Special Love to Leannah's Five Grandsons...

Lee, Luke and Len Allen Holland, *Tyler, Texas*

Will and Foster Smith, *Huntsville, Alabama*

The End

A hostess is like a duck...
calm and serene on top of the water,
and paddlin' like crazy beneath!

ORDER FORMS

The Three E's to Entertaining: Easy, Economical and Enjoyable

MAIL TO: Leannah P. Holland
3606 Provident Court, Mobile, Alabama 36608

Please send me ____ books @ $15.95 each $________
Postage and handling @ $3.00 each $________
AL residents add 4% sales tax @ $ .64 each $________
TOTAL enclosed $________

Name ______________________________
Address ______________________________
City ____________________ State ______ Zip ____________
Please make checks payable to: Leannah P. Holland

The Three E's to Entertaining: Easy, Economical and Enjoyable

MAIL TO: Leannah P. Holland
3606 Provident Court, Mobile, Alabama 36608

Please send me ____ books @ $15.95 each $________
Postage and handling @ $3.00 each $________
AL residents add 4% sales tax @ $ .64 each $________
TOTAL enclosed $________

Name ______________________________
Address ______________________________
City ____________________ State ______ Zip ____________
Please make checks payable to: Leannah P. Holland

Rice?
What to prepare?
Roast?
Potatoes?
Ham?
???
???
Happy Anniversary
Potatoes